# kitchen essentials

# seasonal food

## HOW TO ENJOY FOOD AT ITS BEST

**SUSANNAH BLAKE**

DUNCAN BAIRD PUBLISHERS

LONDON

**For my father, in memory of his allotment**

kitchen essentials
# seasonal food
Susannah Blake

First published in the United Kingdom
and Ireland in 2007 by
Duncan Baird Publishers Ltd
Sixth Floor
Castle House
75-76 Wells Street
London W1T 3QH

Conceived, created and designed by Duncan Baird Publishers

Managing Editor: Grace Cheetham
Editor: Cécile Landau
Managing Designer: Manisha Patel
Studio photography: Diana Miller
Photography assistant: Danielle Wood
Food stylist: Linda Tubby
Food stylist assistant: Rosie Nield
Prop stylist: Róisín Nield
Illustrator: Peter Duggan

British Library Cataloguing-in-Publication Data:
A CIP record for this book is available from the British Library

ISBN: 978-1-84483-368-9

10 9 8 7 6 5 4 3 2 1

Typeset in Interstate and Bergell
Colour reproduction by Colourscan, Singapore
Printed in Singapore by Imago

Publisher's Note: While every care has been taken in compiling the recipes in this book, Duncan Baird Publishers,
or any other persons who have been involved in working on this publication, cannot accept responsibility for any
errors or omissions, inadvertent or not, that may be found in the recipes or text, nor for any problems that may
arise as a result of preparing one of these recipes.

# Contents

# in season

So why do most cooks urge us to try to eat food that is in season? Surely we should rejoice in being able to eat anything we want at any time of the year? Who would not relish fresh strawberries in the depths of winter and asparagus in autumn? Why should we wait until summer to enjoy fresh tomatoes and what is wrong with eating aubergines in spring? Well, the answer is quite simple - it basically boils down to taste, looking after the environment and cost.

With very few exceptions, such as medlars, the vast majority of fresh fruits and vegetables have a far superior taste if they are eaten as soon after picking as possible - having been left to to ripen naturally, of course. Although the differences are not too marked for some produce, for others, such as sweetcorn and peas, they are huge. A forkful of peas or a bite from a corncob, picked a week earlier, packed in plastic and flown across the world, will leave you with a mouthful of mealy, almost tasteless starch. Eat either, plucked fresh from the garden and cooked within minutes, and you will enjoy juicy vegetables, bursting with sweetness and full of vibrant flavours.

If flavour is one of your key concerns - which it probably is if you are reading this book - then you should aim to eat locally grown produce that is in season, so that your food spends as little time as possible between the land and your plate. Eating food that was picked days or weeks ago and has been flown or trucked thousands of miles will never taste as good, no matter how well it is stored and transported. And there are environmental factors to consider too. With our planet warming up and the polar ice caps melting, should we really be eating food that encourages the excessive burning of fossil fuels simply to get it into our kitchens? It surely makes far more sense to eat food that tastes better, helps to support the local economy and makes less of a negative impact on our environment.

Cost is another positive reason for eating local produce while it is in season. You should make the most of foods when they are available in abundance. While they are plentiful, they will be far cheaper than when they are scarce or have been flown in from the other side of the world. If you find cherries on the greengrocers' shelves at the beginning of spring, they are likely to have a high price tag and will not have the marvellous sweet and tangy flavour of those that have had weeks upon weeks of sunshine to ripen them. So why not wait a couple of months? Then you will able to enjoy a huge and affordable bowl of cherries while they are at their very best. Most of the time, eating seasonally is really just common sense.

**NOTES**

I am not suggesting, however, that those who live in the northern hemisphere should eschew tropical fruits and vegetables entirely, or that those in cooler climes should never eat an orange again – but that you try to strike a balance by aiming to eat locally and seasonally most of the time. To stop eating imported foods entirely could have a significant impact on the economies of many nations, particularly those in the developing world. Try to stick to imported foods that simply cannot be grown locally and, wherever possible, buy "fairtrade" produce for which the growers have received a fair price. What you choose to eat can have a far-reaching impact on so many people. Thinking just a little more about what you put on your plate can help to improve the quality of life for whole communities.

## greater choice

You might assume that aiming to eat whatever is in season from month to month will limit your choice and leave you feeling deprived. But, bizarrely, you may find the exact opposite is true. By trying to buy seasonally, you may end up selecting unfamilar foods and actually introducing greater variety into your diet. Despite the wide choice offered by supermarkets all year round, most people have slowly been reducing the range of foods they eat. With the same fruits and vegetables constantly found on the shelves, we have become less adventurous, sticking to what is familiar and producing a virtually identical shopping list week after week. Tomatoes, courgettes, lettuces, broccoli and apples go into the trolley regardless and meals begin to follow a rigid pattern.

By losing our sense of seasonality, we have stopped working with nature's rhythms and have tried to create our own. But often there is no rhythm to what we create. There are no highs and lows, no change, no variety. Many of us seem to have found ourselves with a culinary flatline, in which mealtimes have ceased to be about delicious food at its best and have become just another household chore that requires the minimum of thought and yields the minimum pleasure.

With seasonality, you are forced to make changes, discover new recipes and actually look forward to an old favourite coming into season. What can be better than gorging yourself on asparagus or apricots in the brief couple of months when they are in season? Overindulge in them, because they will not be around for another nine or ten months. Savour every fruit or vegetable as it comes into its season, then move on and enjoy whatever appears next. Every month, new and wonderful produce will arrive on the shelves – so why not make the most of it while it is plentiful and at its very best?

Compare a tomato reared on little else but water in the depths of winter with a glorious, fat, ruby-red one, ripened naturally in the sun throughout the summer and picked at the beginning of autumn. The difference is marked and unmistakable. Why would you wish to make do with the pappy, tasteless winter tomato, when you could relish the sweet, succulent summer variety just a few months later? And it is not even a question of deprivation. The colder months also offer a whole gamut of tasty produce to enjoy in the meantime, from crinkly savoy cabbages and nutty Brussels sprouts to luscious leeks and hearty roots.

Eating seasonally can bring ingredients that you have never tried before into your life, or remind you of ones that you have forgotten about. One of the great pleasures of writing this book has been rediscovering old favourites of my own, such as Jerusalem artichokes and kale, as well as finding ones that have become a joyous addition to my repertoire. Why, for example, have I been passing by kohlrabi for years? It may look a little odd, but it is delicious and easy to prepare, and I can barely wait for it to be back in season again. Even as I write, I feel a little excited at the prospect of picking up a basketful and taking them home to enjoy as soon as I can.

# using the book

The seasons can be fluid and unpredictable. The months in which particular foods arrive can vary according to the weather in any given year as well as from region to region. The sun-soaked Mediterranean will frequently see produce much earlier than, for example, the cooler countries of northern Europe. And in the United States of America and Australia, where there are many different climate zones, ranging from the tropical to the more temperate and even polar conditions, the same produce may enjoy several different seasons within the same country. Also some fruits and vegetables, such as pomegranates, citrus fruits and avocados, can only be grown in warmer places, while others, such as quinces, flourish better in cooler climates.

Little produce fits neatly into any single season, often arriving in one and fading in another. Some, such as apples, carrots and beetroot, keeps well and is available from cold-storage long after it has been harvested. So you can still enjoy fresh and locally grown produce, even though it is officially no longer "in season".

**NOTES**

For the sake of simplicity, the various ingredients covered in this book have been placed in the season or seasons in which they are available in the table on page 219, while they have been divided up according to the season in which they are at their best for the rest of the book. Within the entry for each ingredient, there is detailed information as to when it comes into season and when it is likely to be unavailable. Use this as a basic guide rather than a rigid rule, but, more importantly, stay in touch with what is going on locally.

As a general rule of thumb, the best way to enjoy fresh, seasonal ingredients is to look out for them in your local greengrocer's, farmers' market or farm shop. If you always try to buy fresh, locally grown produce – by default, it should be in season. If you are in your greengrocer's and the place of origin is not marked, ask. A good greengrocer will be happy to help and, if you show interest, will always be pleased to point out what is best on the shelves at any particular time. Local-box schemes are a good bet too – with a weekly delivery of locally grown fruit and vegetables. Some farms may also offer pick-your-own boxes, so you will know exactly how long your food has taken to get from the ground to your plate.

And of course, for avid gardeners, growing your own is a fabulous way to enjoy truly fresh food. But a word of warning – there is a potential downside to this type of enterprise too. If you are champing at the bit to get going on your own seasonal vegetable patch, do spend a little time planning your planting and harvesting carefully to ensure you can enjoy a reasonable variety of food, and avoid gluts of produce all arriving at the same time. When I was a child, my father was a keen gardener with an allotment, which meant I had a wonderfully varied diet, far, far richer than that of most of my school friends. After all, who else got to enjoy a plateful of asparagus every night in late spring and early summer, just hours after it had been picked? However, when a bowl brimming with fresh raspberries was presented for the fortieth time one summer, I began to lose my relish. After the raspberry glut of 1979, I was almost into adulthood before I was able to really enjoy a dish of those glorious fruits again. So you actually *can* have too much of a good thing!

# cooking and its natural rhythms

Throughout time, cuisines have developed around the world founded on the seasons, combining ingredients that are available at the same time to make dishes which suit the weather. And as each new ingredient was introduced from faraway lands and cultivated in its new home, so would it be assimilated into the cuisine. From such a history comes a wonderful heritage of recipes that we can still enjoy and use to help take advantage of today's seasonal produce.

It is no coincidence that throughout the world the same ingredients are frequently found together in recipes. Fresh mint, for example, is a common flavouring for both peas and lamb. The herb enhances the taste of both, but part of the reason that such a combination is so popular is that the ingredients involved come into season at a similar time. In Morocco, Italy and Greece, you will find numerous classic dishes in which artichokes and peas are braised or stewed together, with new potatoes being another regular addition – an obvious mix, when you think of how their seasons overlap. In France, they like to braise lettuces and peas together, with a hint of zesty mint – the perfect light accompaniment on a hot summer day. From Greece and Turkey, through the Middle East and into India, cucumber, yogurt and mint are another classic blend, whether it is in *tzatziki*, *cacik*, *raita* or one of the other numerous similar dishes. Cucumbers and mint are available in abundance at the same time and bring out the best in each other.

Look at the foods we enjoy in spring. After a harsh winter of sturdy, strongly flavoured brassicas, starchy roots and warming stews and roasts, the days grow longer and temperatures begin to rise, and with them the shoots and leaves of the new year. So it makes sense that these tender, delicately flavoured morsels should now be savoured. Freshly picked asparagus is cooked until tender to enjoy with just a little melted butter or hollandaise sauce for dipping. Artichokes are unwrapped leaf by leaf, as the succulent flesh is sucked off each one, until you reach the creamy heart in the centre. Surely it is no coincidence that we make such a sensuous drama of enjoying these fresh new pickings after a season of cold and austerity? Think of all the tender spring leaves as they arrive to provide light salads, perked up with punchy spring onions and fresh herbs, or the excitement of tart, pink rhubarb for turning into pies and fools and crumbles – a refreshing addition to the dessert menu after the apples and pears and dried fruits of winter.

**NOTES**

It is not just the ingredients that have their natural rhythms, but our approach to them works with the seasons too. Spring is the time to relish the arrival of all things new, and marks a move away from the sustaining, warming and comforting dishes that feel so necessary in winter. In contrast, summer makes the most of all those sweet and juicy, crisp and tender, sun-ripened fruits and vegetables - with lighter dishes, including wonderful chilled soups and desserts, to suit the hot weather. And summer dishes make the most of the seasonal abundance that generally accompanies a rise in temperature. Those Mediterranean classics that thrive in the warm sunshine are teamed together: tomatoes, courgettes, aubergines and red peppers sit side-by-side again and again in salads and stews: from French *ratatouille* and Turkish *turlu turlu* to the Middle Eastern salad *fattoush* and Italian *panzanella*. In autumn, dishes warm up again - not only in temperature but in their flavours and textures too - sweet, meltingly soft roast squashes, plum tarts, game cooked with autumn fruits and luscious, earthy wild mushrooms. Dishes are served up that make the most of the rich harvest that was slowly moving towards maturity during the the long, sultry days of summer.

Until fairly recently, what people ate has always been guided by the seasons. It is only lately that summer blueberries have been paired with autumn and winter game, that asparagus has been appearing on Thanksgiving and Christmas canapés and that rhubarb and raspberries have become a classic partnership. Of course, this has only become possible with the effectiveness of freezing certain fruits, vegetables and herbs, and it may be no bad thing when the produce has been frozen at its peak. With summer produce such as tomatoes, this kind of approach can make sense - but for the main why not heed the common sense of eating food at its peak and draw on years of experience by making the most of truly seasonal ingredients?

I am not suggesting for a moment that we should cook and eat only the foods our parents and grandparents did. Cooking offers a wonderful opportunity for constantly developing new flavours, for reworking and experimenting, for allowing one dish to evolve into another - but if the original foundations are solid, why try to replace them with something less firm and secure? A good common-sense approach to successful cooking is to ensure that the basic ingredients of a dish are good; using mediocre ingredients makes it much harder to turn out something fabulous. Make the most of what you have, relish ingredients when they are at their best, draw on the experience of millions of cooks down the centuries and it will be quite difficult to go wrong. But most of all enjoy food for what it is - something natural and delicious.

# the seasonal storecupboard

Throughout the culinary year, you will find yourself relying more or less on storecupboard staples, according to what is in season. For example, in autumn and winter, when you are cooking more substantial dishes, you will probably find yourself using more dried grains, pulses and pasta and relying more on dried fruit, while there is less fresh produce on the greengrocers' shelves. Canned tomatoes, for example, are perfect for stews and soups in winter and spring and are a vast improvement on the tasteless, unseasonal fresh ones that you will find in the shops at that time.

However, whatever the weather and whatever the season, it is always a good idea to keep a well-stocked storecupboard, containing all the basics. You can add to this with your own, or shop-bought, preserved ingredients that have been pickled, bottled, frozen or dried while the fresh ingredients were in abundance and at their best.

## staples

Ingredients such as rice, pasta, beans and other pulses can provide the foundation of many meals – whether a summer salad, hearty winter stew or warming autumnal risotto. It is worth keeping a bag of long-grain rice (quick-cook, basmati, white or brown – it is up to you), as well as one of creamy risotto rice, in the cupboard. With pasta, make sure you have a packet of long pasta such as spaghetti or linguine, and a packet of short pasta, such as penne or fusilli. Beans and pulses are another useful standby. Keep some canned as well as dried ones, as they can save time on soaking and boiling. Other useful staples include couscous, bulghur wheat, lentils, flour (plain, self-raising and strong bread flour, if you're inclined to make your own bread), raising agents such as baking powder, and sugar (brown, white and icing).

## oils and vinegars

Every cook should have in the cupboard a bottle of olive oil and a bottle of sunflower or vegetable oil – essential for sautéeing, frying, roasting and dressings. Aim also to have a bottle each of balsamic vinegar, white-wine vinegar and red-wine vinegar. You can flavour oils and vinegars by adding sprigs of herbs such as tarragon, thyme or rosemary, or spices such as coriander seed or chilli.

**NOTES**

## spices, herbs and other flavourings

Although many spices can be grown only in warmer climates, they are an essential in any kitchen. Most are dried and have a long shelflife, so it is worth investing in a good variety. Basics include cumin, coriander seed, chilli, paprika, turmeric, cardamom, ginger, cinnamon, nutmeg and peppercorns. Store them in a cool, dark place and remember that whole spices retain their flavour longer than ground ones. Dried herbs are a useful standby, but many do not retain their flavour well. Frozen herbs offer a more authentic flavour out of season – particularly the more delicate, tender herbs such as basil, parsley and coriander – so, if you can, freeze your own while they are in season. Other useful flavourings include mustards (Dijon and wholegrain) and sauces such as soy sauce, sweet chilli sauce, fish sauce and Tabasco sauce.

## fresh herbs

Fresh herbs are not strictly a storecupboard ingredient, but to enjoy them at the peak of their flavour it is well worth trying to grow your own if you can – whether it is in a tub on a roof-top terrace, in a corner of the garden or on a sunny windowsill. Generally, this requires little skill and, apart from the superior flavour that home-grown herbs bring to dishes, using them is so much cheaper than buying a bunch of fresh ones every time you need them. Hardier herbs, such as rosemary, thyme, chives, sage and mint, are very easy to grow, although the more delicate varieties, such as basil, coriander and tarragon can prove more difficult, so you may prefer to buy these as and when you need them. Alternatively you can buy them already growing in a pot, and if you keep them on a sunny windowsill, they should thrive.

## preserving seasonal ingredients

One of the best ways to enjoy seasonal ingredients throughout the year is by preserving them while they are abundant and at their best, by making them into jams, jellies, pickles or chutneys.

**STERILIZING, SEALING AND LABELLING PRESERVES:** When making jams, jellies and other preserves, it is essential to sterilize your jars before you fill them and then to seal them properly. They should then be left until the contents have cooled, when a label should be attached, stating clearly what each jar contains, along with the date.

There are various ways to sterilize jars and lids. The easiest is to use a dishwasher. Put the jars and lids in the dishwasher and run it on its hottest setting. Alternatively, put the jars and lids in a large pan and pour hot water in and around them to cover. Bring to the boil and boil for 10 minutes, before leaving to drain upside down.

Different preserves can be sealed in different ways. After potting, sweet jams and jellies can be covered with a wax-paper disc, then the neck of the jar sealed with cellophane, held in position with an elastic band, or sealed with a screwtop lid. Acidic chutneys and relishes should be sealed with non-metallic lids (as the vinegar in them corrodes metal). Bottled fruits and pickled vegetables can be sealed in clamp-top jars with rubber seals.

**MAKING JELLIES:** Clear, sparkling jellies are made by boiling fruit with water, then straining off the juice through a jelly bag or muslin and boiling it with sugar (usually 450g/1lb sugar to every 600ml/1 pint/2½ cups juice) to a temperature of 105°C/220°F. Depending on the fruit, they may be served as an accompaniment to roast meats or as a sweet preserve on buttered toast, on scones spread with cream cheese, or in an American-style peanut butter and jelly sandwich.

To make redcurrant jelly (this method can also be used as a guide for other fruits), strip 900g/2lb redcurrants from their stalks and place in a heavy pan with 400ml/14fl oz/1⅔ cups water. Bring to the boil and simmer gently for about 30 minutes, stirring occasionally, until the fruit is very soft. Gently squash the fruit with the back of the spoon, then pour the fruit and juices into a sterilized jelly bag suspended over a large bowl and leave to drain until juice stops dripping from the bag. (Do not squeeze the bag to speed the process, as this will result in a cloudy jelly.) Measure the juice collected in the bowl into a clean pan and add 450g/1lb sugar for every 600ml/1 pint/2½ cups juice. Heat gently, stirring until the sugar dissolves, then bring to the boil and boil rapidly to a temperature of 105°C/220°F. Remove from the heat, skim off any scum, pour into sterilized jars and seal. Leave to cool, label clearly and store in a cool, dark place.

**MAKING JAMS:** Softly set jams and sweet fruit preserves are delicious spread on bread, toast, scones and muffins and can be used to fill cakes. They are particularly good made with soft summer fruits, such as berries, cherries, currants, apricots and peaches. They are usually made with similar weights of fruit and sugar. You may need to add a little water or fruit juice to less juicy fruits such as peaches and apricots.

**NOTES**

To make raspberry jam (this method can also be used as a basic technique for other fruits, although you will need to add an extra teaspoon of lemon juice when using low-pectin fruits, such as strawberries and cherries), put 450g/1lb raspberries and 1 teaspoon lemon juice in a large pan, place over a low heat, until the juices begin to run, then allow to simmer gently for about 10 minutes. Crush the fruit with the back of a spoon and add 450g/1lb sugar. Stir over a low heat until the sugar has dissolved, then bring to the boil and boil rapidly, stirring occasionally, until the temperature reaches 105°C/220°F. Remove from the heat and skim off any scum. Pour into sterilized jars and seal. Leave to cool completely, label and date the jars clearly and store in a cool, dark place.

**BOTTLING FRUITS:** Preserving fruits in alcohol is a quick, simple and delicious way to enjoy them throughout the year, long after their season has ended. Fruit that has been treated in this way is excellent served with ice cream and other creamy desserts, such as panna cotta and cheesecake, and the richly flavoured liqueur can be strained and enjoyed on its own.

The recipe that follows for bottling soft summer fruits is based on the classic German preserve *rumtopf*, in which different fruits would be added to the jar as and when they came into season. Prepare 900g/2lb summer fruits, such as strawberries, cherries, blueberries, raspberries, blackcurrants and redcurrants, by hulling, pitting and removing the stalks as required and cutting any larger fruits into bite-size pieces. Put all the fruit into a large bowl, sprinkle over 225g/8oz caster sugar, cover and leave to stand for about 1 hour. Spoon the fruit, along with any juices that have formed, into a sterilized preserving jar and pour about 1 litre/ 1¾ pints/4 cups rum over the top to cover. Cover the top of the jar with clear film, then seal and store in a cool dark place for about 2 months before serving.

**MAKING PICKLES, CHUTNEYS AND RELISHES:** Preserved with salt and vinegar, these are good for serving with cold meats and cheeses and in sandwiches. Chutneys and relishes have a more jam-like consistency, while the ingredients used in pickles are usually left whole or halved and are preserved in a flavoured vinegar. Once pickles, chutneys or relishes have been opened, they should be stored in the fridge.

The recipe that follows is for a fruity peach chutney, but a similar technique can be used for other fruits and vegetables, such as mangoes and tomatoes. Put 500ml/17fl oz/2 cups red-wine

NOTES

vinegar in a large pan with 280g/10oz light brown sugar, 150g/5½oz sultanas, 1 teaspoon ground cinnamon and 1 teaspoon ground allspice and heat gently, stirring, until the sugar dissolves. Bring to the boil, then add 450g/1lb peaches that have been peeled, pitted and roughly chopped, 3 sliced onions, 2 green chillies that have been deseeded and chopped, 3 crushed cloves garlic, 2 teaspoons freshly grated root ginger and 1 teaspoon salt. Return to the boil, then reduce the heat and leave to simmer, stirring frequently, for about 45 minutes until the chutney is thick. Spoon into warmed sterilized jars, seal and leave to cool before labelling. Keep in a cool place for at least 2 weeks before serving.

## drying seasonal ingredients

Many seasonal ingredients can be successfully dried so that you can enjoy them at a later date. Drying may alter the flavour of some foods, but not necessarily in a bad way. Ingredients that are particularly well suited to drying include mushrooms, chillies and herbs.

**DRYING MUSHROOMS:** Many wild mushrooms such as ceps (porcini), chanterelles and morels can be dried, then rehydrated by soaking in warm water for about 30 minutes before cooking. Drying tends to intensify the taste of mushrooms and a few added to a risotto or stew made with cultivated mushrooms can give the flavour a real boost.

The simplest way to dry most mushrooms is to slice them, arrange them on a tray in a single layer and then leave them a warm place for several days until dry. They should be stored in an airtight container until ready to use.

**DRYING CHILLIES:** Use dried chillies whole, crumbled into dishes, or rehydrated before use. Drying is an excellent way to preserve fresh chillies if you grow your own. Simply spread them out on a tray in a single layer and leave in a warm place for several days to dry. Store in an airtight container until ready to use.

**DRYING FRESH HERBS:** Although freezing fresh herbs retains much more of their flavour, drying is also a good way of preserving them for later use. Home-dried herbs usually have a better flavour than commercially dried ones. Spread the leaves out on a tray in a single layer and leave in a warm place for several days until dry. Store in an airtight container until ready to use.

## freezing seasonal ingredients

The invention of the freezer has been a boon for the keen cook. Many fresh ingredients freeze incredibly well, so they can be enjoyed later in the year when they are no longer in season. Ingredients that are particularly worth freezing include fresh herbs, soft summer fruits, and vegetables such as corn and peas that deteriorate in flavour rapidly after picking. It is also worth cooking certain ingredients while they are readily available and cheap, as well as preparing and freezing certain dishes for later use. Make use of the abundance of sweet, juicy tomatoes in summer by preparing a huge pan of fresh tomato sauce and freezing it for use in recipes during the cooler months of the year. Poached fruits such as plums and apricots also freeze well and can make a wonderful treat in winter, when the choice of fresh fruit is limited.

**FREEZING SUMMER FRUITS:** Soft summer berries and currants freeze well and can be the focus of wonderful desserts in autumn and winter, when they are no longer in season. Freezing, however, will affect their texture, so they are best used in desserts such as summer pudding, crumbles or pies, in which the fruit is cooked. To freeze these fruits, prepare them by hulling and stripping off stems as required, then spread them out on a baking sheet lined with greaseproof paper. Freeze, then transfer to freezer bags or containers for long-term storage.

**FREEZING HERBS:** Freezing is a great way to preserve the delicious flavour of fresh herbs, particularly delicate ones such as coriander and basil. Frozen herbs, however, are not really suitable for garnishing and are best used for stirring into cooked dishes. There are numerous methods of freezing herbs, but the simplest one is to chop the herbs, then place them in an airtight container in the freezer. They freeze in a loose mass, so you can remove a teaspoonful or so at a time, as and when you need them.

**NOTES**

# Spring

From tender stems of asparagus and the first crunchy carrots of the year to earthy

new potatoes and glorious purple sprouting broccoli, spring marks the end of the

winter chill, a move towards warmth and sunshine and the sprouting of all things

new. Spiky artichokes, crisp spring onions, long pink sticks of tangy rhubarb,

fragrant spring herbs and a wonderful array of succulent young leaves - from sorrel,

nettles and dandelion leaves to peppery rocket and the first lettuces of the year -

all provide a welcome change after the sturdy cabbages, leeks and cauliflowers

of winter. With the new season's lamb comes an exciting array of sheep's milk

cheeses, with their creamy texture and distinctive tart flavour. Many wild

mushrooms may now be out of season, but the delicious morel, with its eye-

catching honeycombed cap, provides a real gourmet treat. Its delicious smoky

taste marks it out as ideal for sautéeing in butter or cooking with a creamy sauce

and serving on polenta wedges - a wonderful base for their intense flavour.

# spring herbs

After the robustly flavoured herbs of autumn, such as rosemary and sage, and the dried herbs of winter, the arrival of an abundance of fresh, tender, aromatic herbs in spring marks a whole new turn in the culinary calendar. Long, thin, oniony chives are wonderful snipped into salads, sprinkled into omelettes and stirred into risottos. They add a freshness that cooked onions can barely touch upon, along with a vibrant splash of colour. Aromatic dill, with its unmistakeable aniseed flavour, is delicious paired with cream and eggs, and is particularly good with fish. Sharp, zesty mint adds an uplifting tang to countless dishes, both sweet and savoury. Try it tossed into salads, dressings and desserts, or sprinkled over Middle Eastern and Asian dishes. Mint really is one of the most versatile of the spring herbs and its powerful fragrance seems to mirror all that is fresh and new about the season. Then there is plenty of parsley too, and marjoram and oregano, both adding the distinct aromas that are so redolent of the Mediterranean kitchen.

## Marinated chicken with tabbouleh

**SERVES 4**
4 skinless chicken breasts
1 clove garlic, crushed
juice of 1 lemon
¼ tsp dried chilli flakes
1 tbsp olive oil

**FOR THE TABBOULEH**
100g/3½oz bulghur wheat
salt and freshly ground black pepper
15g/½oz fresh mint leaves, chopped
60g/2oz fresh flat-leaf parsley, chopped
2 tomatoes, peeled, seeded and diced
2 tbsp olive oil
juice of 1 lemon

Arrange the chicken in a single layer in a shallow dish. Whisk together the garlic, lemon juice, chilli and olive oil, then season with salt and pour over the chicken breasts, turning them to coat well. Cover and leave in the fridge to marinate for at least 1 hour.

Preheat the oven to 220°C/425°F/Gas 7. Put the bulghur wheat for the tabbouleh in a bowl, add a pinch of salt and pour over enough boiling water to cover. Leave to soak for 20 minutes until tender. Drain well, then set aside.

Put the chicken breasts on a baking sheet, pour over the marinade and bake in the oven for 20 minutes, until cooked.

Meanwhile, toss together the drained bulghur wheat with the chopped herbs and tomatoes in a large bowl. Drizzle over the olive oil and lemon juice and season to taste with salt and pepper. Serve with the hot chicken.

NOTES

# Risotto with spinach and spring herbs

**This risotto is a moreish combination of some of the best spring has to offer - a creamy blend of rice and tender young spinach leaves, infused with aromatic dill and chives.**

**SERVES 4**

1.2 litres/2¾ pints/4¾ cups vegetable stock
25g/1oz butter
1 onion, finely chopped
2 cloves garlic, finely chopped
280g/10oz risotto rice
185ml/6fl oz/¾ cup white wine
250g/9oz baby spinach leaves
50g/1¼oz Parmesan cheese, grated, plus extra for sprinkling
handful of fresh dill, chopped
4 tbsp chopped fresh chives
salt and freshly ground black pepper

Pour the stock into a saucepan and bring to the boil. Reduce the heat and keep at a very low simmer.

Melt the butter in another large pan. Add the onion and garlic and cook gently over a medium heat for about 5 minutes, until soft. Add the risotto rice and cook, stirring, for another 2 minutes.

Pour in the wine and simmer, stirring continuously, until all the liquid has been absorbed. Add a ladleful of the hot stock and continue to simmer, stirring, until the stock has been absorbed. Continue cooking in this way for about 18–20 minutes, until the rice is almost tender and most of the stock has been used up.

Stir in the spinach and cook for a further 1–2 minutes until the leaves are tender and wilted. Remove the pan from the heat, stir in the grated Parmesan and chopped dill and chives and season to taste with salt and pepper. Serve immediately, with extra Parmesan sprinkled over.

# Herb salad with sheep's milk cheese

**SERVES 4**

1½ tbsp cider vinegar
3 tbsp olive oil
½ tsp sugar
2 tsp finely chopped fresh mint
salt and freshly ground black pepper
3 large handfuls of spring salad leaves, such as rocket, lollo rosso and baby beetroot leaves
large handful of fresh herbs, such as coriander, parsley, sorrel and chives
2 apples
100g/3½oz sheep's milk cheese, such as Pecorino or Manchego, shaved into thin slices

Whisk together the cider vinegar, olive oil, sugar and mint in a small bowl to make a dressing. Season to taste with salt and pepper and set on one side.

Put the salad leaves and herbs in a large serving bowl and toss together to combine.

Core the apples and cut into wedges. Scatter these, along with the cheese shavings, over the salad leaves and herbs. Drizzle with the prepared dressing and toss to mix well.

Serve immediately.

# Lamb skewers with mint salsa (opposite)

**SERVES 4**

500g/1lb 2oz lean lamb, trimmed and cut into 2.5cm/1in cubes
2 cloves garlic, crushed
2 tsp ground cumin
2 tbsp red-wine vinegar
1 tbsp olive oil
salt and freshly ground black pepper

**FOR THE MINT SALSA**

1 cucumber, peeled, seeded and diced
1 tomato, peeled, seeded and diced
3 tbsp chopped fresh mint leaves
handful of fresh flat-leaf parsley, chopped
3 spring onions, thinly sliced
¼ tsp sugar
1 tsp white-wine vinegar
1 tbsp olive oil

Put the cubes of lamb into a large bowl. Whisk together the garlic, cumin, vinegar and olive oil in a small bowl, then season to taste with salt and pepper. Pour this mixture over the lamb, toss to coat, cover and leave to marinate in the fridge for at least 2 hours.

To make the salsa, mix together the cucumber, tomato, chopped mint and parsley and spring onions in a serving bowl. In a separate bowl, stir the sugar into the vinegar until it has dissolved, then whisk in the olive oil and season to taste with salt and pepper. Pour over the cucumber, tomato and herb mixture and toss to combine. Check the seasoning and add more salt or pepper if necessary. Set aside and keep cool until ready to use.

Preheat the grill to hot. Remove the lamb from the fridge and thread the cubes of meat on to 8 skewers. Place under the grill for 8-10 minutes, turning halfway through the cooking time, until well browned and cooked to your liking. Serve with the salsa.

# Grilled salmon with lemon and dill sauce

**Tangy and brimming with the fragrance of fresh dill, the simple creamy sauce, served here with salmon, will make a good match for any type of grilled or baked fish.**

**SERVES 4**

4 salmon fillets or steaks, around 200g/7oz each
salt and freshly ground black pepper
6 tbsp mayonnaise
1½ tsp Dijon mustard
3 tbsp lemon juice
1½ tsp grated lemon rind
4 tbsp finely chopped fresh dill
pinch of caster sugar

Preheat the grill to hot. Season the salmon with salt and pepper, then place under the grill for about 6 minutes, turning halfway through the cooking time, until just cooked through.

While the fish is grilling, put the mayonnaise, mustard and lemon juice and rind into a bowl and whisk together until smooth and creamy. Stir in the dill, then add the sugar and season to taste with salt and pepper. Serve this sauce with the freshly grilled fish.

**NOTES**

# spring leaves

Tender young leaves, sprouting from the earth along with the other spring shoots, are a refreshing seasonal treat after the hardier greens of winter. The first lettuces - the succulent round variety and the sweet little gems and romaines - arrive, making a perfect base for a host of light, healthy salads. They are delicious combined with the freshly unfurled leaves of other spring plants, such as spinach, rocket, watercress, beetroot and even wild nettles and dandelions, creating a delightful mix of colours and flavours. The torn leaves of tangy lemony sorrel also make a wonderful zesty addition to the salad bowl and can give an extra lift to soups and sauces, especially those to go with fish and poultry. And there are spring greens, too, sometimes known as collard greens. A type of kale, their dark green leaves are picked before a heart forms, or may be grown as a special non-heart-forming variety. They can be cooked and served in the same way as the curly winter variety and make a delicious accompaniment to roast spring lamb.

## Smoked mackerel fishcakes with sorrel sauce

**SERVES 4**
450g/1lb smoked mackerel fillets
450g/1lb potatoes, boiled
2 spring onions, trimmed and finely chopped
salt and freshly ground black pepper
2 tbsp plain flour
1 egg, beaten
150g/5½oz dried breadcrumbs
oil, for frying

**FOR THE SORREL SAUCE**
125ml/4fl oz/½ cup white wine
125ml/4fl oz/½ cup double cream
large handful of sorrel (about 100g/3½oz), finely shredded

Remove the skin from the mackerel and flake the flesh into a large bowl. Mash the potatoes, then add to the mackerel with the spring onions and stir to mix. Season with black pepper, then shape the mixture into 8 round patties.

Heap the flour on to a plate. Dip each patty into the flour to coat, then dip in the egg and roll in the breadcrumbs until well covered. Place in the fridge to chill for about 20 minutes.

Meanwhile make the sauce. Put the wine and cream in a pan and heat to a gentle simmer. Stir in the sorrel until just wilted. Season to taste with salt and pepper and set aside and keep warm while cooking the fishcakes.

Heat the oil in a frying pan. Add the prepared fishcakes and fry for about 3 minutes on each side until crisp and golden. Drain on kitchen paper and serve with the sauce poured over.

**NOTES**

# Chilled spring-leaf soup

**Sorrel gives this soup a lovely lemony tang, while rocket lends it a peppery bite. You can use other spring leaves such as nettles in place of some of the rocket and spinach, but keep the quantity of sorrel the same because it really does add an essential zing.**

**SERVES 4**

225g/8oz potatoes, diced
1 litre/1¾ pints/4 cups vegetable stock
2 bunches spring onions, trimmed and sliced
140g/5oz spinach, roughly shredded
55g/2oz rocket, roughly shredded
85g/3oz sorrel, roughly shredded
200ml/7fl oz/generous ¾ cup white wine
125ml/4fl oz/½ cup double cream
salt and freshly ground black pepper

Put the potatoes and stock in a large pan, bring to the boil, then reduce the heat, cover and simmer for about 10 minutes until the potatoes are tender.

Add the spring onions, spinach, rocket and sorrel, cover and simmer for about 2 minutes until the leaves are wilted.

Pour the soup into a food processor or blender and blend to a smooth purée. Stir in the wine and cream. Season to taste with salt and pepper, leave to cool, then place in the fridge to chill for at least 2 hours before serving.

# Linguine with rocket pesto

**Peppery rocket makes a great alternative to basil in this fresh green pesto. You can substitute the pinenuts for other nuts such as hazelnuts or almonds if you like.**

**SERVES 4**

300g/10½oz linguine
salt and freshly ground black pepper
40g/1½oz pinenuts
1 clove garlic, chopped
2 large handfuls of rocket
4 tbsp olive oil
55g/2oz Parmesan cheese, grated, plus extra to serve

Cook the linguine in a pan of boiling salted water according to the instructions on the packet. Drain well, reserving about 4 tablespoons of the cooking water.

Meanwhile, prepare the pesto. Put the pinenuts, garlic, rocket and olive oil in a food processor and process until smooth, then stir in the grated Parmesan cheese.

Add the pesto and 3-4 tablespoons of the reserved cooking water to the freshly cooked pasta. Toss well to combine, then season with plenty of black pepper. Serve immediately, sprinkled with more grated Parmesan cheese.

**NOTES**

# Mixed-leaf salad with seared beef and garlic dressing

**The peppery bite of wasabi, a relation of horseradish, gives this fresh, fruity spring salad a real kick – perfect with tender, juicy, seared beef.**

**SERVES 4**

250g/9oz piece sirloin beef
4 tbsp olive oil
1 clove garlic, crushed
1 tsp wasabi paste
1 tbsp cider vinegar
pinch of sugar
2 tsp finely chopped fresh mint leaves
salt
115g/4oz mixed spring leaves, such as rocket, baby spinach and nettles
2 pears, peeled, cored and cut into thin wedges
handful of hazelnuts, toasted and chopped

Trim off any fat or sinew from the meat and brush with about ½ tablespoon of the oil. Heat a griddle pan until very hot, brush with a little more of the oil, then press the meat down on it for about 2 minutes. Flip over and cook for a further 2 minutes, then cook for a further 2 minutes on each side, or until cooked to your taste. Lift on to a board, cover with foil and leave to rest for 10 minutes.

Meanwhile, whisk together the garlic, wasabi, vinegar, sugar and remaining oil. Stir in the mint and season to taste with salt. Set aside.

Arrange the leaves on four serving plates and scatter the pear wedges and hazelnuts over the top. Slice the beef thinly and scatter over the salad, then drizzle with the dressing and serve.

# Spring greens with lemon and garlic

**Buy only loosely packed heads of spring greens that are crisp and deep green with no signs of yellowing. As with other members of the cabbage family, they should be cooked until just tender, retaining some bite – avoid overcooking at all costs.**

**SERVES 4**

2 heads of spring greens, finely shredded
salt and freshly ground black pepper
2 tbsp olive oil
2 cloves garlic, finely chopped
juice of 1 lemon

Plunge the shredded greens into a pan of boiling salted water for 2-3 minutes until just tender. Drain well.

Meanwhile, heat the oil in a large frying pan, add the garlic and gently fry for about 1 minute. Toss in the drained greens and season to taste with salt and pepper. Stir in the lemon juice and serve immediately.

# spinach

Although it is available for most of the year, spinach is one of the highlights of spring. Then its tender young leaves make such a refreshing change after the sturdy greens and hearty roots of winter. First cultivated in Persia, but now a staple of cuisines worldwide, spinach is a versatile vegetable. The soft baby leaves can be used raw in salads or make a lovely addition to risottos, stir-fries and even mashed potato; larger leaves, sautéed with a little garlic, then seasoned and served with a squeeze of lemon, make a delicious accompaniment to grilled meats and fish.

Spinach has a natural affinity with butter, cheese, cream and eggs, but is also delicious matched with various herbs and spices. In India, a blend of spiced spinach and potato is often served with rice or flatbreads. In Spain, it is cooked with garlic, raisins and pinenuts to make a popular tapas dish, while in the Middle East it is added to stews and used in fillings for pies and pastries.

Choose fresh-looking leaves, and avoid any that are yellowing, wilting or becoming slimy. Cut off tough stems and always wash well in cold water to remove any soil or grit. Then shake off as much water as possible, patting the leaves dry on kitchen paper if necessary, before cooking in a dry, tightly covered pan for a few minutes, until they have wilted. Spinach gives off a lot of liquid while cooking, so always drain well before serving or using in a recipe.

## Baby spinach and new potato salad with melting Gorgonzola (opposite)

**SERVES 4**
600g/1lb 5oz new potatoes
salt and freshly ground black pepper
1 tbsp balsamic vinegar
2 tbsp olive oil
½ tsp wholegrain mustard
115g/4oz baby spinach
150g/5½oz Gorgonzola cheese, cut into bite-size pieces

If the potatoes are on the large side, cut into bite-size pieces. Add to a pan of boiling salted water and cook for about 10 minutes until tender. Drain well.

Meanwhile, prepare a dressing by whisking together the vinegar, olive oil and mustard in a small bowl. Season to taste with salt and pepper, then set aside.

Arrange the spinach leaves on four serving plates and scatter the Gorgonzola cheese over the top, followed by the hot potatoes. Drizzle over the dressing, toss to combine and serve immediately.

**NOTES**

# Spanakopitta

**SERVES 6**
2 tbsp olive oil
1 onion, finely chopped
500g/1lb 2oz spinach
3 large eggs
200g/7oz feta cheese, drained
and crumbled
handful of fresh dill,
roughly chopped
freshly ground black pepper
about 140g/5oz filo pastry sheets
40g/1½oz butter, melted

Preheat the oven to 190°C/375°F/Gas 5. Grease a 20 x 25cm/ 8 x 10in baking dish.

Heat the oil in a large pan. Add the onion and gently fry for about 5 minutes, until soft. Meanwhile, wash the spinach well and shake off as much water as possible. Stir the spinach into the onion, cover and cook for about 5 minutes, stirring occasionally, until wilted. Remove from the heat and drain well, squeezing out as much liquid as possible, then leave until cool enough to handle. Roughly chop the spinach leaves.

Beat the eggs in a bowl, add the feta and dill and season well with black pepper. Add the spinach and stir to combine thoroughly.

Line the baking dish with three layers of filo pastry, brushing each sheet with butter as you go, and allowing the sheets to hang over the edge of the dish. Spread the spinach filling in an even layer over the filo, then fold up the overhanging pastry over it. Top with another three layers of filo, brushing each sheet with butter.

Using a sharp knife, mark the top with a diamond pattern, then bake in the oven for about 35 minutes, until crisp and golden. Serve warm or cold.

# Spinach and nutmeg soup

**SERVES 4**
25g/1oz butter
2 small onions, chopped
1 potato, chopped
1.2 litres/2¼ pints/4¾ cups
vegetable stock
500g/1lb 2oz spinach
125ml/4fl oz/½ cup double cream
pinch of freshly grated nutmeg
juice of ¼ - ½ lemon
salt and freshly ground black pepper

Melt the butter in a large pan, then add the onions and gently fry for about 4 minutes until soft. Add the potato and vegetable stock. Bring to the boil, then reduce the heat, cover and simmer for about 15 minutes, until the potatoes are tender.

Meanwhile, wash and drain the spinach. Add to the pan and cook over a gentle heat for about 3 minutes, until it has wilted.

Tip the contents of the pan into a blender or food processor and process until smooth. Return to the pan and heat through gently. Stir in the cream, then add the nutmeg and lemon juice and season to taste with salt and pepper. Serve.

**NOTES**

# Garlicky spinach with raisins and pinenuts

**SERVES 4**

1 tbsp raisins
2 tbsp olive oil
6 tbsp pinenuts
3 cloves garlic, finely chopped
500g/1lb 2oz spinach, washed and dried
salt and freshly ground black pepper

Place the raisins in a bowl, pour over boiling water and leave to soak for about 10 minutes. Drain well and set aside.

Heat the oil in a pan, add the pinenuts and gently fry for 2-3 minutes until golden. Add the garlic and cook for about 30 seconds, being careful not to let it burn.

Add the spinach to the pan and toss over the heat for about 3 minutes, until it has wilted. Stir in the raisins, season to taste with salt and pepper and serve immediately.

# Roast monkfish on creamy garlic spinach

**SERVES 4**

1 monkfish tail (about 500g/1lb 2oz)
2½ cloves garlic
¼ lemon, sliced into half-rounds
2 sprigs of fresh rosemary
salt and freshly ground black pepper
about 2 tbsp olive oil
25g/1oz butter
600g/1lb 5oz spinach, washed and dried
3 tbsp double cream
pinch of freshly grated nutmeg
lemon wedges, to serve

Preheat the oven to 220°C/425°F/Gas 7. Remove any membrane from the monkfish tail and cut down either side of the central bone to create two fillets.

Finely slice 1½ of the garlic cloves and sprinkle over the cut side of one of the monkfish fillets, top with the half-slices of lemon and then with the sprigs of rosemary. Place the second fillet, cut-side down, on top to form a fish-fillet 'sandwich'. Tie together at intervals with string to hold securely. Season well with salt and pepper.

Heat about 1 tbsp of the oil in a frying pan. Add the monkfish 'sandwich' and fry for about 2-3 minutes on each side until browned. Transfer to a baking dish, drizzle with a little more oil and roast in the oven for 15-20 minutes until cooked through.

About 5 minutes before the end of the cooking time, melt the butter in a saucepan. Chop the remaining garlic and gently fry in the butter for about 1 minute. Add the spinach and cook, stirring, for about 2 minutes until wilted. Stir in the cream and nutmeg and season to taste with black pepper.

Remove the string from the fish and slice thickly. Serve on top of the creamy spinach, with lemon wedges for squeezing over.

# asparagus

Tender fresh asparagus, with its mild yet distinctive flavour, is one of the great joys of spring, lasting right through into early summer. The green variety is the most common, with stems that can vary in size from fine spears only a few millimetres thick to sticks as sturdy as your thumb. You will also come across white and purple-tinged asparagus.

Usually eaten as an appetizer – served warm with melted butter, vinaigrette or hollandaise sauce – the cooked spears are also a wonderful addition to salads, tarts, layered terrines, risottos, pasta and even scrambled eggs. They make an attractive and delicious topping for canapés, such as bruschetta and crostini, too.

Asparagus is best eaten on the day it is picked, so it is ideal if you can grow your own or buy it locally from somewhere you know it has been freshly picked. Farm shops are often a good source. Imported asparagus can be tough and lacking in flavour. Look for firm green spears with tightly packed buds, and avoid any that are withered or beginning to brown.

## preparing and cooking asparagus

Asparagus spears can be cooked in numerous ways, but the simplest method is to cook them in simmering water until just tender. They can then be eaten with your fingers, accompanied by a dip of melted butter or hollandaise sauce.

Some cooks recommend using an asparagus steamer to cook the spears. This is a tall pan with a basket inside to hold the spears upright, so that when the pan is filled with boiling water, the stalks cook in the water, while the delicate tips steam above it. However, it is just as effective to cook asparagus lying flat in a frying pan containing about 2.5cm/1in of simmering water. Cooking time will depend on the thickness of the spears. If they are thin and delicate, they will become tender in a couple of minutes, while thicker stems may need 6–8 minutes. The best way to test if asparagus is cooked is to lift a spear out with a fish slice and take a bite. It should be tender and juicy, but not soft.

To prepare asparagus, rinse lightly under cold running water, then snap off the end of each stem – it should pop and break just where the stem ceases to be woody and becomes tender. Pour about 2.5cm/1in water into a large frying pan and bring to the boil. Arrange the asparagus in the pan in a single layer and cook over a gentle-medium heat until tender. Then carefully lift out of the pan using a fish slice or spatula and pat dry on kitchen paper before serving.

**NOTES**

# Roast asparagus wrapped in pancetta

**SERVES 4**

200g/7oz thin green asparagus
16 wafer-thin slices pancetta,
cut into 5-7cm/2-3in strips
olive oil, for drizzling
freshly ground black pepper

**FOR THE LEMON MAYONNAISE**

8 tbsp mayonnaise
juice and grated rind of 1 lemon
small handful of fresh dill,
finely chopped

Preheat the oven to 190°C/375°F/Gas 5.

Prepare the lemon mayonnaide in a small serving bowl by mixing together the mayonnaise, lemon juice and rind and the chopped dill. Cover and place in the fridge.

Wrap each asparagus spear in a strip of pancetta. Arrange on a baking sheet and drizzle over the olive oil. Sprinkle over a little black pepper and roast in the oven for 6-7 minutes until tender.

Serve warm with the bowl of lemon mayonnaise.

# Asparagus risotto

**SERVES 4**

800g/1lb 12oz asparagus, trimmed
825ml/1½ pints/3⅓ cups
vegetable stock
25g/1oz butter
1 onion, finely chopped
280g/10oz risotto rice
185ml/6fl oz/¾ cup vermouth
25g/1oz Parmesan cheese, grated,
plus extra for sprinkling
large handful of fresh flat-leaf
parsley, chopped
1 tsp chopped fresh mint leaves
salt and freshly ground black pepper

Pour about 2.5cm/1in water into a large frying pan and bring to the boil. Lower the heat, arrange the asparagus in the pan in a single layer and then leave to simmer for about 4 minutes until just tender. Drain, reserving the cooking water. Refresh the spears in cold water, then cut into 5cm/2in pieces, separating the tips from the stems.

Heat the vegetable stock with the aparagus cooking water in a large pan. Leave to simmer gently.

In a separate pan, melt the butter, then add the onion and cook gently for about 4 minutes until soft. Add the rice and cook, stirring, for 2 minutes. Pour in the vermouth and cook, stirring, until all the liquid has been absorbed. Add a ladleful of the stock and cook, stirring, until it has been absorbed. Continue cooking and adding stock in this way for about 10 minutes.

Stir in the asparagus stems and continue cooking and adding stock for about 8 minutes. Add the asparagus tips and cook for a further 2 minutes, until the rice is tender and creamy

Remove the pan from the heat and stir in the Parmesan and chopped herbs. Season to taste and serve with extra Parmesan.

# artichokes

There are many different varieties of artichoke, ranging from tiny, delicate specimens to huge giants with heads the size of a small cauliflower. Those that arrive with the coming of spring are the first batch of a long growing season that continues right through summer and well into the autumn. Piled high on market stalls, these magnificent flower-like vegetables, which are related to the thistle, are almost regal in appearance.

Artichokes are a prized ingredient in many parts of the world, but it is the cuisines of the Mediterranean, where they originate, that have really exploited their subtle taste and texture to the full. Cultivated in Italy since the 15th century, they feature in countless classic Italian dishes: deep-fried and served with pasta, sliced and piled on to pizza, cooked in casseroles with lamb and salt cod. In Greece, Cyprus and Turkey, they make a popular side dish, braised with new potatoes and other spring vegetables; and in Morocco they are frequently cooked with preserved lemons and north African spices.

When choosing artichokes look for green, fresh-looking specimens with the stalk still attached, and avoid those with blemishes or dried-out tips. Store them in the vegetable drawer of the refrigerator and use them as soon as possible after purchase.

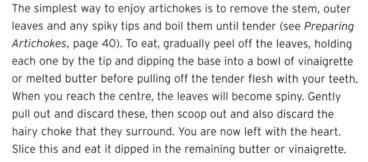

## eating artichokes

The simplest way to enjoy artichokes is to remove the stem, outer leaves and any spiky tips and boil them until tender (see *Preparing Artichokes*, page 40). To eat, gradually peel off the leaves, holding each one by the tip and dipping the base into a bowl of vinaigrette or melted butter before pulling off the tender flesh with your teeth. When you reach the centre, the leaves will become spiny. Gently pull out and discard these, then scoop out and also discard the hairy choke that they surround. You are now left with the heart. Slice this and eat it dipped in the remaining butter or vinaigrette.

**NOTES**

## preparing artichokes

Artichokes are very versatile and can be prepared in many different ways. The simplest is to cut off the woody stem and the tough outer leaves, then snip off the spiky tops of the remaining leaves and boil whole in salted water - for about 10 minutes for baby ones, and 25-40 minutes for larger specimens. To check if an artichoke is cooked, pull off an outer leaf and bite into the fleshly base - it should be really tender. Drain well and serve, warm or cold, with a dip of garlicky vinaigrette or melted butter (see *Eating Artichokes*, page 38).

Artichokes can also be hollowed out, by removing the hairy choke and fleshly heart, to leave a casing of leaves, ready for stuffing. The choke should be discarded, but the heart makes a lovely addition to stews or braised dishes. Some recipes use only the heart, which can be removed from an uncooked artichoke by cutting away the stalk and larger leaves, then pulling off and discarding the inner leaves. Note that, once cut, artichokes will darken. To avoid this, dip them in a bowl of acidulated water (juice of ½ lemon stirred into 1 litre/1¾ pints/4 cups water) from time to time as you work.

# Artichokes dressed in garlic and herbs

**SERVES 4**

4 large artichokes, stems, outer leaves and spiky tips of remaining leaves removed
salt and freshly ground black pepper
grated rind of 1 lemon
1 tbsp lemon juice
1 clove garlic, finely chopped
1 tsp Dijon mustard
pinch of sugar
3 tbsp olive oil
handful of fresh flat-leaf parsley, chopped

Cook the artichokes in boiling salted water for 25-40 minutes until cooked (the fleshy base of leaves should be tender). Drain and refresh under cold water. Pat dry with kitchen paper and set aside.

To make the dressing, whisk together the lemon rind, lemon juice, garlic, mustard, sugar and olive oil and season to taste with salt and ground black pepper. Stir in the parsley and set aside.

Cut the artichokes lengthways into quarters, then use a teaspoon to scoop out the choke and very thin inner leaves. Trim off and discard the woodiest tips of the leaves. Place in a serving bowl, pour over the dressing, toss to coat, then set aside for at least 30 minutes to allow the flavours to come together.

**NOTES**

# Artichokes with chicken and preserved lemon

**SERVES 4**

4 artichokes, stems, outer leaves and spiky tips of remaining leaves removed
3 tbsp olive oil
4 chicken breasts
2 cloves garlic, chopped
2 tsp coriander seeds, crushed
1 preserved lemon, chopped
185ml/6fl oz/¾ cup white wine
salt and freshly ground black pepper
small handful of fresh flat-leaf parsley, chopped
couscous, to serve

Cut each artichoke into quarters lengthways. Remove and discard the choke. Set aside in a bowl of acidulated water (see page 40).

Heat 1 tbsp of the oil in a frying pan. Add the chicken and cook for 1-2 minutes on each side until golden. Set on one side.

Heat the remaining oil in a large saucepan. Add the garlic and cook for 1 minute, stirring. Add the coriander seeds and cook for 30 seconds, then add the drained artichokes, preserved lemon and chicken. Pour over the wine, season with salt and pepper and bring to the boil. Reduce the heat and simmer for about 20 minutes, stirring occasionally, until the artichokes are tender and the chicken is cooked through. Check the seasoning, sprinkle with parsley and serve with couscous.

# Linguine with artichokes and smoked salmon

**The blend of pale green artichoke hearts and pink strips of smoked salmon makes this simple, creamy pasta dish look stunning. Marinated bottled or tinned artichoke hearts may be substituted when fresh artichokes are out of season.**

**SERVES 4**

300g/10½oz linguine
salt and freshly ground black pepper
125ml/4fl oz/½ cup double cream
125ml/4fl oz/½ cup white wine
1 bunch spring onions, shredded
4 large artichoke hearts, cooked (see *Preparing Artichokes*, page 40) and chopped
1 tsp wholegrain mustard
200g/7oz smoked salmon, cut into strips

Cook the linguine in boiling salted water according to the instructions on the packet.

About 3 minutes before the end of the pasta cooking time, put the cream, wine, spring onions, artichoke hearts and mustard in a pan and heat gently, stirring to combine.

As soon as the pasta is cooked, drain well. Stir the smoked salmon into the cream mixture, season to taste with salt and pepper, then pour over the pasta and toss well to combine. Serve immediately.

# purple sprouting broccoli

The short season for purple sprouting broccoli begins in the depths of winter and continues through into spring. This highly attractive vegetable offers a wonderful alternative to the more commonly found blue-green calabrese variety of broccoli (and the less common bright green romanesco) that is found during the rest of the year. Purple sprouting broccoli has long, shooting stems with coarse green leaves and a purple tinge to its heads. With a more delicate flavour than the other broccolis, it makes a wonderful treat. Enjoy it lightly steamed until tender and served as an appetizer with hollandaise sauce or melted butter (rather like asparagus) or use it in tarts, gratins, soups, sauces and pasta dishes, as well as in stir-fries and salads.

When buying, always choose firm stems with tightly packed heads and really fresh-looking leaves. Avoid specimens that are wilting, soft or discoloured. Remove the leaves, trim the ends of the stalks and peel away any thick skin, then either steam or boil until it is just tender and still retains its bite and colour. If stir-frying, cut into bite-sized pieces. If a recipe requires only the florets, do not throw away the stems – when cooked, they are tender and juicy and have a marvellous flavour. Use them in another recipe such as a soup or stew.

## Broccoli and spring onion salad

**SERVES 4**
2 bunches spring onions
2 tbsp olive oil
1.25kg/2lb 12oz purple sprouting broccoli, trimmed
shavings of Parmesan cheese for sprinkling (optional)

**FOR THE DRESSING**
½ tsp grated orange rind
½ red chilli, seeded and chopped
2 tbsp orange juice
1 tsp lemon juice
2 tbsp olive oil
salt and freshly ground black pepper

First make the dressing. Put all the ingredients in a jug, seasoning to taste with salt and pepper, and whisk together. Set aside.

Preheat the grill to hot. Trim the root and tops of the spring onions and strip off the papery outer skin. Arrange on a grill pan. Drizzle with the olive oil and season to taste with salt and pepper. Grill for 3-4 minutes on each side until tender.

Meanwhile, pour about 5cm/2in of water into a wide pan and bring to the boil. Add the broccoli and cook for about 5 minutes, until just tender. Drain well and pat dry.

Divide the broccoli and grilled spring onions between four warm serving plates, drizzle over the dressing and scatter with Parmesan shavings, if using. Serve immediately.

**NOTES**

# spring onions

Spring onions, as their name implies, make their first appearance just as the chill of winter starts to recede and remain available for most of the year. They are immature onions that are harvested only a few months after planting. Creamy white, with fresh green leaves, they can range from long thin stems, about the width of a pencil, to chunky shoots, nearly 1cm/½in thick, with fat bulbous ends. They have a mild sweet flavour – with none of the pungency of fully grown onions – and a lovely crisp texture that reflects the lush freshness that we associate with the spring harvest.

Trimmed and rinsed under cold running water, they can be left whole, cut into lengths, sliced, chopped or trimmed to make curls or brushes and used as a garnish. Raw spring onions will enliven a salad or salsa, but they are also delicious cooked. They require only brief cooking, making them a perfect addition to stir-fries and Asian-style soups, into which they can be tossed at the last minute. The really fat spring onions are wonderful grilled, taking on a mouthwatering sweetness as they become wonderfully succulent and juicy – try serving them with a dip as an appetizer, or tossed into salads.

## Grilled spring onions with bagna cauda

**Brushed with oil, then grilled, spring onions take on a deliciously sweet and mellow flavour, far less pungent than they taste when raw. They make the perfect dipper for munching on with this rich, fragrant, garlicky dip from Italy.**

**SERVES 4**
3 bunches fat spring onions, trimmed
olive oil, for brushing

**FOR THE BAGNA CAUDA**
150ml/5fl oz/²⁄₃ cup extra virgin olive oil
4 cloves garlic, crushed
55g/2oz can anchovy fillets, drained and crushed
85g/3oz butter
freshly ground black pepper

Preheat a griddle pan or grill until hot. Brush the spring onions with olive oil. Place in the griddle pan or under the hot grill and cook for about 3 minutes on each side until tender.

Meanwhile, make the bagna cauda. Gently heat the olive oil and garlic in a pan for 2–3 minutes. Stir in the anchovy fillets and butter and season to taste with black pepper. Put into a serving bowl.

Serve the hot dip immediately with the freshly grilled spring onions. If possible, keep the dip warm at the table by placing it in a fondue pan or in a heatproof dish set over a tabletop warmer.

**NOTES**

# Hot-and-sour soup with spring onions and tofu

**The sweet fresh taste of spring onions shines through in this intensely flavoured broth. Enjoy it as a light starter to a Thai-style meal, or stir in a spoonful or two of plain boiled rice or noodles and serve as a light lunch or supper.**

**SERVES 4**

1.2 litres/2¾ pints /4¾ cups vegetable stock
1 tsp Thai red curry paste
1 tbsp sweet chilli sauce
2 shallots, finely sliced
2 red chillies, seeded and finely chopped
4 kaffir lime leaves, sliced
1 lemongrass stalk, peeled and finely chopped
1 bunch spring onions, trimmed and shredded
2 tbsp Thai fish sauce
juice of 1 lime
about 2 tsp soft brown sugar
300g/10½oz silken tofu, cubed
handful of fresh coriander, chopped

Put the stock, curry paste, sweet chilli sauce, shallots, half the chopped chillies, the lime leaves and lemongrass in a large pan. Bring to the boil, stirring until the curry paste has dissolved, then reduce the heat, cover and simmer gently for 15 minutes.

Strain the stock into a clean pan. Stir in the spring onions, fish sauce, lime juice and sugar to taste. Bring to the boil, lower the heat and leave to simmer for about 1-2 minutes.

Stir in the tofu and cook for a further minute, until the tofu is warmed through and the spring onions are tender. Sprinkle over the remaining chilli and the chopped coriander and serve.

## champ

A classic Irish dish, champ is a mixture of creamy mashed potatoes flavoured with lightly cooked spring onions. It makes a fabulous accompaniment to meat, poultry and fish.

To prepare, cook about 900g/2lb of potatoes in lightly salted boiling water for about 20 minutes until tender. Drain well, allow to steam dry, then mash.

Trim and finely slice 2 bunches of spring onions. Put in a pan with 125ml/4fl oz/½ cup of milk and 55g/2oz of butter. Heat until bubbling gently, then leave to simmer for 2-3 minutes.

Stir into the mashed potatoes with 2 tablespoons of crème fraîche. Season to taste with salt and freshly ground black pepper and serve piping hot.

# garlic

Although available dried at any time of the year, fresh and wild garlic are among the delights of spring. The green young leaves of wild garlic, also known as ramsons, have a powerful and distinctive aroma. Their flavour, however, is no stronger than that of cultivated garlic. They are delicious in salads with other spring leaves, or shredded and added to soups, stews, risottos and omelettes, or wrapped around fish or meat before grilling or roasting. The bulbs can be used in the same way as those of cultivated garlic.

Fresh, greeny-white bulbs of spring garlic do not reach the market until late in the season. They may be pure white or tinged with purple, depending on variety, and have a milder, sweeter flavour than dried bulbs, which makes them ideal for roasting whole and using raw in salads.

Almost every cuisine in the world uses garlic in its recipes, from the fragrant dishes of the Mediterranean to the fiery curries of India and Thailand and the subtly spiced stews of the Middle East. Preparation is all important. The more finely you chop garlic, the more pungent its flavour becomes – so for a milder result cook the bulbs or cloves whole, or for a more intense flavour crush the peeled cloves. The easiest way to peel garlic is to lay a clove on a board and press down on it with the flat side of a knife blade. The papery skin will split and can then be pulled off.

## spaghetti with garlic and chilli

This simple Italian dish known as *spaghetti aglio e olio* is the perfect way to show off garlic at its best.

For four people, cook 300g/10½oz of dried spaghetti in boiling salted water according to the instructions on the packet.

Meanwhile, gently heat 5 tablespoons of olive oil in a frying pan. Add 3 crushed cloves of garlic and 1 dried red chilli and fry for about 2 minutes, until the garlic gives off its aroma and is just starting to brown. Remove from the heat and discard the chilli.

Drain the pasta, stir in the garlicky oil and scatter over a handful of chopped fresh parsley. Toss to combine and serve.

### aioli

This thick, buttery garlic mayonnaise is wonderful served with almost anything – dolloped on new potatoes, asparagus spears or thin florets of purple sprouting broccoli; as a dip with chips or crudités; spread on crostini; or served with salad or poached fish. You can make it at any time of year, but it is at its best prepared with fresh spring garlic. Just combine 2 crushed garlic cloves with 2 egg yolks. Using a hand blender, gradually beat in about 125ml/4fl oz/½ cup of extra virgin olive oil – adding it drop by drop at first, then in a thin drizzle – until the mixture is really thick. Blend in 1 tablespoon of lemon juice and ½ teaspoon of Dijon mustard, then gradually beat in a further 125ml/4fl oz/½ cup of olive oil and season to taste with salt and freshly ground black pepper. Add a little more lemon juice if desired.

# Garlic mussels in white wine

**This simple-to-prepare dish is an absolute classic and is one of the best ways to enjoy garlic as an aromatic seasoning. Eat the mussels first, then mop up the rich, garlicky cooking liquor with chunks of crusty French bread.**

**SERVES 4**

1.8kg/4lb fresh mussels, cleaned
25g/1oz butter
3 cloves garlic, finely chopped
350ml/12fl oz/1½ cups white wine
6 tbsp double cream
large handful of fresh flat-leaf parsley, roughly chopped
salt and freshly ground black pepper
crusty French bread, to serve

Check the mussels, discarding any open ones that do not shut when tapped. Melt the butter in a large pan, add the garlic and gently fry for about 1 minute. Add the mussels, pour over the wine, cover the pan tightly and cook for about 5 minutes until the mussels have opened (discard any that have not opened).

Lift the mussels into warmed serving bowls using a slotted spoon. Quickly stir the cream and chopped parsley into the cooking liquor and season with salt and pepper to taste. Pour over the mussels and serve with the crusty French bread.

**NOTES**

# Chicken with forty cloves of garlic

**Garlic can be used as a vegetable in its own right, roasted whole to produce a sweet, mellow result - and you can easily allow a whole bulb per person without the flavour being overwhelming. Cooked in this way, the flesh becomes mild, fragrant, smooth and buttery and can be squeezed out of the papery skin. Roast cloves of garlic make a delicious partner for roast chicken, as in this recipe, but are also good simply spread on to crusty bread or thin slices of warm toast and eaten as a snack.**

**SERVES 4-6**

1 lemon
1.6kg/3½lb free-range chicken
4-6 sprigs of fresh thyme
25g/1oz butter
salt and freshly ground black pepper
5 bulbs garlic
2 tbsp olive oil
240ml/8fl oz/1 scant cup chicken stock
2 tbsp white wine

Preheat the oven to 200°C/400°F/Gas 6.

Cut the lemon in half and rub the cut ends all over the chicken, then place the lemon halves in the cavity of the bird along with the thyme. Rub the butter all over the breasts and legs and season well with salt and pepper. Place the chicken in a roasting tin.

Remove the papery outer layers of skin from the garlic bulbs, leaving them whole, then slice off the very tops to expose the cloves. Place the bulbs on a large sheet of foil, drizzle over the oil, season with a little salt and pepper, then fold up the foil tightly around them and place in the roasting pan next to the chicken.

Roast in the oven for 45 minutes. Remove from the oven and unwrap the garlic, disposing of the foil. Tuck the garlic in around the chicken, drizzling over any juices that have formed. Return to the oven and cook for a further 15 minutes until golden. Insert the point of a knife into the thickest part of the thigh - if the juices run clear, the chicken is cooked; if not, return to the oven for a further 15 minutes, then check again. Transfer the cooked chicken and garlic to a board and leave to rest for 10 minutes.

Meanwhile, make the gravy. Skim off the fat from the juices left in the roasting tin and discard, then pour the juices into a blender. Squeeze the flesh from 2 of the bulbs of garlic and also add to the blender. Pour in the chicken stock and wine and process until smooth. Pour into a saucepan, heat through and serve with the chicken and remaining roasted garlic bulbs.

# avocados

Native to South America, the avocado grows in most tropical regions of the world. With different varieties coming into season at different times, they are available most of the year – but their fresh flavour and delightful, pale green, buttery flesh seems so at home on the spring table with the green, tender shoots and stems of that season. Colour, flavour and texture vary according to variety. The skin ranges from bright green and shiny to purple-black and knobbly, but all types have a rich, creamy flesh.

Avocado flesh is fabulous in salsas or tossed into salads and makes a good, enriching addition when blended into soups and smoothies. However, it starts to blacken quite quickly once exposed to the air, so prepare avocados only shortly before serving. Squeeze lemon juice on any leftover avocado and cover closely with clear film to prevent it discolouring.

## Avocado salad with spicy seared prawns (opposite)

**SERVES 4**
2 tbsp sweet chilli sauce
1 tsp soy sauce
juice of 1 lime
1 clove garlic, crushed
275g/9½oz raw tiger prawns, peeled (leaving tails on) and deveined
115g/4oz mixed spring leaves, such as rocket, baby spinach and nettles
2 avocados, peeled, stoned and cut into bite-size chunks
4 spring onions, trimmed and sliced

**FOR THE DRESSING**
juice and grated rind of 1 lime
1½ tsp soft brown sugar
2 tbsp sunflower oil
½ red chilli, seeded and chopped
2 tsp chopped fresh mint leaves
salt

Combine the chilli sauce, soy sauce, lime juice and garlic in a bowl. Add the prawns, toss to coat, then leave in the fridge to marinate for at least 30 minutes.

Meanwhile, whisk together the dressing ingredients in a bowl or jug, seasoning to taste with salt. Set aside.

Divide the salad leaves among individual serving plates or bowls. Scatter the avocado chunks and spring onions over the leaves, then drizzle over about two-thirds of the dressing and toss to coat the leaves.

Preheat a ridged griddle pan or grill until hot, and use to cook the prawns, with any marinade poured over, for about 1–2 minutes on each side, until pink and cooked through. Scatter the hot prawns over the plates of salad, drizzle over the remaining dressing and serve immediately.

**NOTES**

# rhubarb

"Forced" rhubarb – cultivated in dark sheds to encourage the stems to grow in the search for light – arrives at the end of winter. Naturally grown rhubarb appears in early spring and lasts to the beginning of summer. It is brighter in colour with a stronger flavour than the forced variety and makes a real treat, as one of the first of the seasonal fruits to reach the market.

Choose forced rhubarb with firm pink stems and no trace of green or soft slimy patches. Naturally grown rhubarb is green and pink-red in colour, but again go for stems that are firm and fresh-looking. To prepare, cut off and discard the leaves and woody stem tips, then strip out any tough strings and cut into chunks. Simmer in a covered pan with sugar and very little water, or sprinkle with sugar and bake.

## Rhubarb meringue pie

**SERVES 6**
300g/10½oz rhubarb, trimmed and chopped
1 tsp ground cinnamon
150g/5½oz caster sugar
2 eggs, separated

**FOR THE PASTRY**
115g/4oz plain flour
½ tbsp caster sugar
60g/2¼oz butter, chilled and diced
about 1 tbsp cold water

First make the pastry. Put the flour and sugar in a food processor and pulse to combine. Add the butter and process until the mixture resembles fine breadcrumbs. With the machine running, add just enough water for the mixture to come together. Lightly press the pastry into a ball, wrap in clear film and chill for about 30 minutes.

Preheat the oven to 190°C/375°F/Gas 5. Put the rhubarb, cinnamon and 3 tablespoons of the sugar in a pan, cover and heat gently, shaking occasionally, until the juices flow. Increase the heat slightly and simmer for 6-8 minutes until the rhubarb is tender. Off the heat, beat in the egg yolks, one at a time, then allow to cook gently, stirring, for 2-3 minutes until thickened. Set aside.

Roll out the pastry to line a 20cm/8in tart tin, cover with foil and scatter over baking beans and bake in the oven for 10 minutes. Remove the beans and foil, then bake for a further 5-10 minutes until crisp and golden. Meanwhile, whisk the egg whites to form stiff peaks. Fold in the remaining sugar, a spoonful at a time, to make a meringue.

Pour the rhubarb mixture into the tart case and spread out in an even layer. Swirl the meringue on top, then bake for 20-25 minutes until golden. Serve hot or warm.

# carrots

Although carrots that have been kept in cold-storage are available at almost any time, the first carrots of the year arrive at the end of spring, with the main harvest at the end of summer or early autumn. These sweet, bright-orange roots are delicious eaten raw or cooked. Sliced, chopped, grated or cut into thin sticks or batons, they can be transformed into wonderful salads or added to soups, stews, curries and even some desserts. In India, grated carrots are cooked slowly with milk, sugar and spices to make that wonderful, sticky, fudgy sweet, *halwa*. They are also excellent boiled and mashed with swedes, turnips or potatoes and plenty of butter, or roasted along with a selection of other root vegetables, or juiced with a knob of fresh root ginger, then served up blended with orange or apple juice.

When buying carrots, look for firm unblemished specimens, ideally with fresh-looking leaves attached. Look out too for those that have been organically grown, as they tend to have the best flavour. If using organic carrots, just trim and scrub well to prepare, leaving the skins on, as this is where much of the flavour resides. Non-organic carrots are best peeled.

Carrots are best cooked in very little liquid, so that all their flavour stays inside rather than being lost into the cooking liquid. The simplest way is to slice them thinly and cook in a covered pan with just a splash of water, a knob of butter and a good grinding of salt and pepper, until tender and sweet. If there is any liquid left in the pan when the carrots are cooked, increase the heat and cook uncovered, stirring, until it has all evaporated.

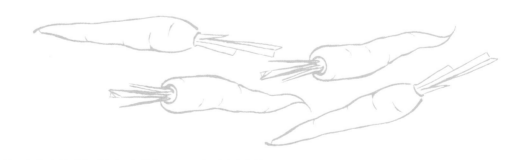

**NOTES**

# Sea bass baked on gingered carrots

**Baking carrots brings out their intense sweetness, which is enhanced and balanced here by the addition of pungent fresh ginger and the zesty tang of fresh lime juice. This creates a strongly flavoured bed of vegetables that is the perfect foil for the mild-tasting sea bass.**

**SERVES 4**

4 sea bass fillets, about 175g/6oz each
salt and freshly ground black pepper
juice of 2 limes
2 tbsp sunflower oil
1 onion, finely chopped
1 clove garlic, crushed
2.5cm/1in piece fresh ginger, peeled and grated
675g/1½lb carrots, grated

Preheat the oven to 220°C/450°F/Gas 7. Season the fish well with salt and pepper, sprinkle over the lime juice and set aside.

Heat the oil in a large pan. Add the onion, garlic and ginger and fry gently for about 5 minutes until soft. Add the carrots and cook, stirring, for about 5 minutes until just tender. Remove from the heat. Pour in the lime juice from the fish and season to taste with salt and pepper.

Transfer the carrot mixture to a baking dish, then arrange the fish fillets in a single layer on top, skin side up. Bake in the oven for about 10 minutes until the fish is just cooked through.

## moroccan-style carrot dip

Cooked carrot salads, flavoured with warm spices such as cumin, ginger and chilli, are popular throughout North Africa. This aromatic, fiery-coloured dip has similar flavourings and is great served with wedges of pitta bread for scooping, either on its own as an appetizer or as part of a selection of snacks or *mezze* nibbles, such as hummus, stuffed vine leaves and olives.

To make, just peel and slice 450g/1lb of carrots and put in a pan with 3 tablespoons of cold water, then bring to the boil, lower the heat and simmer gently for 25-30 minutes, shaking the pan from time to time, until the carrots are soft. If there is still cooking liquid in the pan, increase the heat and bubble, stirring, until most of it has evaporated.

Transfer the cooked carrots to a food processor with 1½ chopped garlic cloves, 1 teaspoon of grated fresh ginger, a good pinch of cayenne pepper, 1 teaspoon each of ground cumin and ground coriander, 1 tablespoon of red-wine vinegar, 2½ tablespoons of olive oil and a good pinch of salt.

Process to a form a smooth purée, check the seasoning and add a little more salt and cayenne pepper if needed. Scoop into a bowl and chill well before serving.

# Carrot and cardamom cake *(opposite)*

**Carrots have a natural affinity with warm spices such as ginger, cinnamon and cardamom, and their intense sugary flavour makes them an ideal candidate for sweet dishes and desserts. Stirred into cake batter, they produce a deliciously moist cake that keeps well.**

**MAKES 1 LARGE CAKE**
100g/3½oz soft brown sugar
55g/2oz caster sugar
250ml/9fl oz/1 cup sunflower oil
3 eggs
grated rind of 1 orange
seeds from 10 cardamom pods, crushed
½ tsp ground ginger
300g/10½oz self-raising flour
2 large carrots, grated (about 225g/8oz total grated weight)
85g/3oz walnuts, chopped

**FOR THE ICING**
250g/9oz mascarpone cheese
grated rind of 1 orange
2 tsp lemon juice
55g/2oz icing sugar

Preheat the oven to 180°C/350°F/Gas 4. Grease a 19cm/7½in round cake tin and line with greaseproof paper.

Beat together the sugars, oil and eggs in a large bowl, then stir in the orange rind, cardamom seeds and ginger. Sift over the flour and carefully fold in, then fold in the grated carrots and walnuts. Tip the mixture into the prepared cake tin and spread out evenly. Bake for 1-1¼ hours in the oven, until a skewer inserted in the centre comes out clean. Turn out on to a wire rack and leave to cool completely.

To make the icing, beat together the mascarpone, orange rind, lemon juice and icing sugar. Spread over the cooled cake. Serve cut into wedges.

## baked carrots

This simple technique produces a similar result to cooking carrots in a pan with very little water. Allow 1-2 carrots per person. Cut them into batons or diagonal slices and place in the centre of a large square of foil. Season to taste with salt and freshly ground black pepper, dot with a knob or two of butter and drizzle over ½-1 tbsp of vermouth (per serving). Wrap the foil around the carrots and twist the ends to make a well-sealed parcel. Place on a baking tray and bake in a preheated oven at 190°C/375°F/Gas 5 for 15-20 minutes, until sweet and tender. If liked, sprinkle over a handful of freshly chopped seasonal herbs just before serving.

# new potatoes

Although potatoes are available all year round and are a common staple in many national cuisines, the arrival of tiny new potatoes in spring is a real treat. Sweet and tender, most varieties are best eaten in their skins, where much of their nutritional value and flavour lies.

When buying, choose unblemished potatoes that are still covered in muddy soil. Wash well, removing any bad spots, but never peel them. Larger new potatoes can be halved, but leave the smaller ones whole. Then simply boil in salted water for about 15 minutes, or until tender.

With their waxy flesh, boiled new potatoes are perfect for using in salads - either warm or cold. Try tossing them, fresh from the pan, into a bowl of baby spinach, along with chunks of Gorgonzola cheese; the heat of the potatoes will wilt the leaves and melt the cheese, producing a sublimely indulgent dish. Or boil and lightly crush the potatoes, then serve with a sprinkling of freshly chopped spring herbs and a drizzle of extra virgin olive oil; or parboil, then toss in olive oil, sprinkle with sea salt and roast until crisp.

## New potatoes cooked with onion and garlic

**SERVES 4**
25g/1oz butter
1 onion, finely chopped
2 cloves garlic, finely chopped
675g/1½lb new potatoes, halved
salt and freshly ground black pepper
4 tbsp water
handful of fresh flat-leaf parsley
or chives, chopped

Melt the butter in a pan. Add the onion and garlic and cook gently over a low heat for about 4 minutes, until soft. Add the potatoes, season to taste with salt and pepper, toss to combine, then pour in the water and cover the pan tightly.

Leave to simmer gently, shaking the pan from time to time, for about 15 minutes, until the potatoes are tender and the liquid reduced. Check the level of liquid in the pan towards the end of cooking and add a splash more water if too dry. Toss in the chopped herbs, check the seasoning and serve.

**NOTES**

# Chicken and new potato stew with chorizo and sherry

**SERVES 4**

2 tbsp olive oil
4 chicken breasts or legs, about 200g/7oz each
1 onion, halved and sliced
2 cloves garlic
60g/2¼oz chorizo, diced
400g/14oz can chopped tomatoes
125ml/4fl oz/½ cup dry sherry
pinch of dried chilli flakes
salt
450g/1lb new potatoes
handful of fresh flat-leaf parsley, chopped

Heat the oil in a large flameproof casserole or wide pan, add the chicken and brown all over. Remove from the pan and set aside.

Reduce the heat under the pan, add the onion and garlic and cook for about 5 minutes, until soft. Add the chorizo and cook for 2 minutes, then add the tomatoes, sherry and chilli flakes and season with a little salt.

Add the browned chicken and the potatoes to the pan, bring to the boil, then reduce the heat, cover and leave to simmer gently for 25–30 minutes, stirring occasionally, until the chicken is cooked through and the potatoes tender. Check the seasoning and serve sprinkled with the chopped parsley.

## new potato salad

Cooked in their skins, bite-size new potatoes, with their wonderful waxy texture and earthy flavour, are perfect for making into potato salad. This recipe can be served warm or at room temperature.

For four, allow about 675g/1½lb of potatoes. Scrub clean, cut any large ones in half, then cook in boiling salted water for about 10 minutes until tender. Drain well and leave to steam dry.

Meanwhile, make the dressing. Pound 2 peeled garlic cloves in a mortar, then work in 1 teaspoon of Dijon mustard and about 1½ tablespoons of sherry vinegar. Whisk in 4 tablespoons of extra virgin olive oil, a handful of fresh flat-leaf parsley and a few sprigs of fresh mint, both finely chopped. Season with plenty of freshly ground black pepper and a little salt.

Pour the dressing over the cooked potatoes, toss to mix in thoroughly and serve.

# morels

Morels – unlike most other wild mushrooms which appear in the autumn – are a springtime delicacy. Pale brown, with creamy white flesh, their wrinkly pointed caps resemble a sponge. The short stems are hollow inside and should always be split and rinsed under cold running water to remove dirt and dust before using. Morels have an intense aroma and flavour that goes particularly well with butter and cream, and are considered a real gourmet treat. They make a good addition to risottos and sauces.

Morels should never be eaten raw and generally require longer cooking than other mushrooms. First split them in half and wash as described above, then sauté in butter for about 30 minutes until tender and juicy. If you are lucky enough to find yourself with a glut of morels, they can be threaded on string and dried, then stored in an airtight container. Soak dried morels in warm water for about 20 minutes before cooking.

## Creamy morels on polenta wedges (opposite)

**SERVES 6**
25g/1oz butter
1 large clove garlic, crushed
225g/8oz fresh morels, or a mixture of morels and cultivated mushrooms, cleaned (see above)
3 tbsp white wine
salt and freshly ground black pepper
2 tbsp double cream
handful of fresh flat-leaf parsley, chopped, plus extra for sprinkling

**FOR THE WEDGES**
500ml/17fl oz/2 cups water
125g/4½oz quick-cook polenta
butter, for frying

First make the wedges. Bring the water to the boil in a large pan, add a pinch of salt and then the polenta, stirring constantly. Continue cooking for about 3 minutes until the mixture is really thick, then turn out on to a wooden board in a mound, flatten down slightly until about 1cm/½in thick and leave to cool and set. When set, cut into six wedges and set aside.

Melt the butter in a clean pan, add the garlic and fry gently for 1 minute. Add the mushrooms and wine, season with a little salt and cook over a low heat for 25 minutes, stirring occasionally, until tender and the liquid has evaporated. Stir in the cream and parsley and season to taste with salt and pepper.

Melt a little butter in a frying pan (with a ridged base, if available), add the prepared wedges and fry on both sides until crisp and golden. Top each one with a spoonful of the mushrooms, sprinkle on a little extra parsley and serve immediately.

NOTES

# lamb

Lamb is available at any time of the year, but the sweet, succulent, tender meat from animals aged between 4 and 12 months is traditionally associated with spring. Simply roasted with garlic and rosemary, and served with mint sauce, new potatoes and carrots, lamb makes a truly special seasonal feast.

But it is not just the roasting joints, such as the leg, shoulder, saddle, loin and rack, that can be enjoyed in spring; there is also a fabulous choice of smaller cuts that can be pan-fried or grilled for a quick, easily prepared weekday meal. Try loin and chump chops, or tender leg steaks, noisettes or ribs. Tougher cuts, such as shank and neck, make wonderful stews and cubed or minced lamb is perfect in pies, stuffed vegetables and baked dishes, such as *moussaka*.

When choosing lamb, look for firm pink meat with a firm-grained texture and creamy white fat. Avoid dark, grainy or dry-looking meat, or meat with yellowing fat.

## marinades for lamb

One of the best ways to prepare small cuts of lamb, such as leg steaks, chops and noisettes, is to marinate them for at least 1 hour in the fridge, then grill or pan-fry. Simple marinades include:

2 crushed cloves of garlic mixed with 2 tablespoons of red-wine vinegar, a few sprigs of chopped fresh thyme or oregano and 1 tablespoon of olive oil, then seasoned with salt and black pepper.

2 crushed cloves of garlic mixed with the juice of 1 lemon, 2 teaspoons of ground cumin, 1 teaspoon of ground coriander, 1 tablespoon of olive oil, and salt and black pepper to taste.

2 crushed cloves of garlic mixed with ½ finely chopped onion, a small handful of chopped fresh coriander or mint, 1 teaspoon of chilli powder, 125ml/4fl oz/½ cup of plain yoghurt, and salt and black pepper to taste.

**NOTES**

# Roast lamb with rosemary, garlic and white beans

### SERVES 4-6

250g/9oz dried haricot beans, soaked in cold water overnight
1 leg of lamb, about 1.8kg/4lb
4 cloves garlic, 2 slivered and 2 finely chopped
5 sprigs of fresh rosemary
4 tbsp olive oil
salt and freshly ground black pepper
1 onion, finely chopped
3 rashers of streaky bacon, snipped into small pieces
500ml/17fl oz/2 cups lamb or beef stock
250ml/9fl oz/1 cup boiling water
125ml/4fl oz/½ cup white wine
1 bay leaf

Drain the beans, rinse well and place in a large pan. Cover with cold water and bring to the boil. Boil rapidly for about 10 minutes and skim off any scum that floats to the surface. Reduce the heat and leave to simmer for about 45 minutes, until the beans are just tender, but not soft. Drain and set aside.

Meanwhile, with a small knife, make slits all over the lamb, then press the garlic slivers and leaves from 2 of the rosemary sprigs into the slits. Drizzle about half the oil over the lamb and season well with salt and pepper. Set aside.

Preheat the oven to 190°C/375°F/Gas 5. Heat the remaining oil in a pan, add the onion and chopped garlic and cook over a gentle heat for about 5 minutes, until soft. Add the bacon and cooked beans and toss to combine. Tip the mixture into a large roasting tin or baking dish. Pour over the stock, water and wine and tuck in the remaining rosemary and the bay leaf.

Place the lamb on top of the beans and roast in the oven for about 2 hours, or until the meat is cooked to your liking. Leave to rest for about 15 minutes before carving, keeping the beans warm to serve with the lamb.

# Lamb tagine with dried apricots

### SERVES 4

500g/1lb 2oz lamb shoulder, cut into 2.5cm/1in cubes
1 onion, thinly sliced
2 cloves garlic, chopped
pinch of ground ginger
1 tsp ground cinnamon
2 tsp ground cumin
2 tbsp olive oil
100g/3½oz ready to eat dried apricots
juice of ½ lemon
salt and freshly ground black pepper
couscous, to serve

Put the lamb, onion, garlic, ginger, cinnamon, cumin and oil in a flameproof casserole, season well and pour over enough cold water to cover. Bring to the boil, then reduce the heat, cover tightly and leave to simmer gently for 1 hour.

Stir in the apricots, then recover and leave to simmer for a further 30 minutes, until the sauce is reduced and the lamb is tender. Stir occasionally towards the end of cooking to prevent the base of the stew from burning, and add a splash more water if it is becoming too dry. Stir in the lemon juice, season to taste with salt and pepper and serve with couscous.

# Summer

Along with rising temperatures comes a wealth of vibrant fresh ingredients that all depend on long days of warmth and sunlight to develop their full flavour. Tender lettuce leaves, crunchy cucumbers, sweet-tasting peas, cobs of golden corn and crisp green beans all mark the arrival of summer, as do offerings associated with the sunny Mediterranean, such as tomatoes, sweet peppers, tender courgettes and fat glossy aubergines. Fruit, too, is one of the glories of the season. After the relative austerity of winter and spring, the arrival of an abundance of glistening summer fruits, piled high on market stalls and greengrocers' shelves, is a pleasure to relish. Juicy cherries, berries in varied tones of red and purple and heavily scented melons ripen to perfection under the sun's rays to achieve their intense sweetness. Velvet-skinned peaches and nectarines just cry out to be bitten into, and the sharp intensity of gooseberries and the honeyed tang of fresh apricots are utterly irresistible, eaten fresh or blended into mouth-tingling purées and mousses.

# summer herbs

As the warmer weather continues into summer, an abundance of fragrant herbs appears. The heady perfume of coriander, mint, basil, tarragon, dill, chives, parsley and marjoram should fill the summer kitchen. Toss into salads or use as flavourings and garnishes for cooked dishes. Create delicious herb butters to dollop on to potatoes or roasted onions or grilled fish and meat. These can be made very quickly and easily: simply chop up a large handful of fresh herbs and blend with a few tablespoons of softened butter, then season with freshly ground black pepper.

## Couscous with summer vegetables and herbs (opposite)

**This simple salad of couscous, sweet roasted vegetables and salty feta cheese, infused with the intense aromas of fresh mint, parsley and basil, makes a wonderful light meal or side dish with grilled meat or fish. Prepare in advance to serve at summer picnics or barbecues.**

### SERVES 4

2 yellow peppers, cut into large chunks
2 red peppers, cut into large chunks
250g/9oz cherry tomatoes
2 courgettes, thickly sliced
5 tbsp olive oil
salt and freshly ground black pepper
1 tbsp white-wine vinegar
1 tsp Dijon mustard
pinch of sugar
200g/7oz couscous
250ml/9fl oz/1 cup boiling water
115g/4oz feta cheese, crumbled
1 tbsp chopped fresh mint leaves
large handful of fresh flat-leat parsley, chopped
handful of fresh basil leaves, torn

Preheat the oven to 200°C/400°F/Gas 6. Put the peppers, tomatoes and courgettes in a large baking dish, drizzle over 2 tablespoons of the oil, season well with salt and pepper and toss to coat. Roast in the oven for about 30 minutes, tossing once or twice, until tender and slightly charred.

Meanwhile, prepare the dressing. Whisk together the vinegar, mustard, sugar and 2½ tablespoons of the oil and season to taste with salt and pepper, then set aside.

Put the couscous in a large bowl, blend in the remaining oil and a pinch of salt using a fork, then pour over the boiling water. Leave to stand for 5 minutes, then fluff up with a fork.

Add the roasted vegetables, with any juices from the dish, and the feta to the couscous, sprinkle over the mint, parsley and basil, then pour over the dressing. Toss to combine well and serve either warm or at room temperature.

**NOTES**

# Pesto with trenette, potatoes and green beans

**SERVES 4**

2 large handfuls of fresh
basil leaves
40g/1½oz pinenuts
1 clove garlic, chopped
4 tbsp olive oil
25g/1oz Parmesan cheese, grated,
plus extra to serve
salt and freshly ground black pepper
300g/10½oz dried trenette or
tagliatelle pasta
about 250g/9oz potatoes, diced
300g/10½oz green beans, trimmed
and halved if long

First make the pesto. Put the basil, pinenuts and garlic in a food processor or blender with 2 tablespoons of the oil and process briefly to mix. Scrape down the sides, add the remaining oil and process further, until smooth. Stir in the Parmesan and season to taste with black pepper. Set aside.

Cook the trenette in a pan of boiling salted water according to the instructions on the packet. Five minutes before the end of cooking time, add the diced potatoes and the beans and cook until tender. Drain well, reserving about 4 tablespoons of the water.

Stir the reserved water into the pesto, then pour the mixture over the pasta and vegetables. Toss to combine and serve immediately, sprinkled with more Parmesan and black pepper.

# Herb-marinated pork steaks

**The tangy Asian-inspired marinade is brimming with the fragrances of lemongrass, lime zest and coriander. Serve this quick-to-prepare dish with a salad of summer leaves, tossed together with ripe tomatoes, crunchy cucumber and a few chunks of ripe peach or mango.**

**SERVES 4**

4 pork loin steaks
2 lemongrass stalks, chopped
2 cloves garlic, crushed
7.5cm/3in piece fresh ginger, peeled
and grated
1 green chilli, seeded and
finely chopped
handful of fresh coriander, chopped
grated rind and juice of 2 limes
2 tsp soy sauce
2 tbsp sunflower oil

Arrange the pork steaks in a single layer in a dish. Combine the lemongrass, garlic, ginger, chilli, coriander, lime rind and juice, soy sauce and oil in a bowl, then pour over the steaks, turning them to coat well. Leave to marinate in the fridge for at least 1 hour.

Preheat the grill to hot. Lift the steaks out of the marinade and arrange on a grill pan. Pour over the marinade, then cook under the grill for about 6 minutes on each side, until just cooked through. Serve immediately.

**NOTES**

# Fish en papillote with summer herbs

**SERVES 4**
2 tbsp olive oil
1 onion, halved and sliced
2 cloves garlic, finely chopped
2 courgettes, cut into batons
2 yellow peppers, cut into strips
salt and freshly ground black pepper
2 handfuls of fresh basil, chopped
1 tbsp chopped fresh mint leaves
4 salmon fillets, about 175g/6oz
each, skinned
juice of 1 lemon

Preheat the oven to 200°C/400°F/Gas 6. Cut out four 35cm/14in squares of greaseproof paper.

Heat the oil in a large frying pan. Add the onion and garlic and fry gently for about 5 minutes until soft. Increase the heat, toss in the courgettes and peppers and cook, stirring frequently, for a further 5 minutes. Remove the pan from the heat, season to taste with salt and pepper, then toss in the basil and mint.

Divide the vegetables among the four sheets of greaseproof paper, placing them in the centre. Lay a salmon fillet on top of each pile of vegetables, sprinkle over the lemon juice and season with salt and pepper. Scrunch up the paper to form a tightly sealed parcel. Place on a baking sheet and bake in the oven for about 15 minutes until the fish is cooked. Serve immediately.

# Herb omelette

**SERVES 2**
4 eggs
handful of fresh flat-leaf parsley,
chopped
1 tbsp chopped fresh chives
handful of fresh basil, chopped
salt and freshly ground black pepper
1 tbsp olive oil

Beat the eggs and chopped herbs together in a large bowl and season well with salt and pepper. Heat the oil in a non-stick frying pan until very hot, then pour in the egg mixture, tilting the pan so that the mixture covers the base.

Cook for a few moments until the egg starts to set, then carefully push in the sides of the omelette to allow any uncooked mixture to run on to the base of the pan. Cook for a further 1-2 minutes, until the egg is just beginning to set on top.

Using a spatula, fold one side of the omelette inwards, then fold the other side over the top of that. Gently cut in half and slide each portion on to a warm serving plate. Serve immediately.

# summer leaves

Summer is the time for lettuces in all their wondrous forms. They are perfect for munching on when the weather is hot and sunny. From pale loose-leafed butterheads and crisp refreshing icebergs to soft leafy lollo rosso, oakleaf and lamb's lettuce and the sweetly flavoured cos and little gems, there is such a huge choice available. And there are also the leaves that give your salads bite and pep, including peppery endive, rocket and watercress and zesty sorrel and wild dandelion. Be adventurous, combining leaves in your salads to create a fabulous array of colours, textures and flavours. Vary them to match the character of other dishes on the table.

## Summer leaves with chargrilled chicken (opposite)

**SERVES 4**

1 clove garlic, crushed
pinch of dried chilli flakes
juice of ½ lemon
4 tbsp olive oil
salt and freshly ground black pepper
4 chicken breasts, about 200g/7oz each, cut into bite-size pieces
1 tbsp red-wine vinegar
1 tsp Dijon mustard
2 tsp chopped fresh mint leaves
2 little gem lettuces
2 small ripe mangoes, stoned, peeled and diced
1 cucumber, sliced

Combine the garlic, chilli, lemon juice and 1 tbsp of the olive oil in a large dish and season with a pinch of salt. Add the chicken, toss to coat well and leave to marinate in the fridge for at least 1 hour.

Meanwhile, make a dressing by whisking together the remaining olive oil, vinegar, mustard and mint in a small bowl. Set aside.

Divide the lettuces into leaves, then tear into bite-size chunks. Divide between four serving plates or salad bowls. Scatter the mangoes and cucumber on top.

Drain the chicken. Heat a griddle pan or grill until hot and use to cook the chicken pieces for about 2 minutes on each side, until cooked through. Scatter the hot chicken over the salad, drizzle over the dressing and toss to combine. Serve.

**NOTES**

### simple leaf salad

Mixing mildly flavoured leaves and flavoursome herbs in a simple salad creates a great accompaniment to summer meals. For four people, combine approximately 115g/4oz of summer leaves, such as lamb's lettuce, oakleaf, lollo rosso and curly endive, in a large salad bowl. Scatter over 2 large handfuls of mixed herbs, such as dill, basil, fennel, mint, chives, coriander and flat-leaf parsley, roughly chopped. (Be sparing with the more intensely flavoured herbs such as mint and chives.) Whisk together 1½ tablespoons of balsamic vinegar, 4 tablespoons of olive oil and 1 teaspoon of wholegrain mustard in a small bowl. Season to taste with salt and pepper, drizzle over the salad and toss to combine. Serve immediately.

# Summer leaf salad with smoked salmon

**SERVES 4**

2 red peppers, halved lengthways
4 lightly smoked salmon fillets, about 140g/5oz each, skinned
salt and freshly ground black pepper
150g/5½oz mangetout
115g/4oz mixed summer leaves, such as rocket, baby spinach and cos lettuce
4 tomatoes, cut into eighths
½ cucumber, sliced
1 tbsp finely chopped fresh mint leaves
juice of 1 lemon
grated rind of ¼ lemon
3 tbsp olive oil

Preheat the oven to 230°C/450°F/Gas 8. Place the peppers, cut side down, on a baking sheet and roast in the oven for about 30 minutes, until blackened all over. Transfer to a bowl, cover with clear film and leave to cool for about 10 minutes. Peel, discard the seeds and cut the flesh into strips. Set aside.

Reduce the oven temperature to 200°C/400°F/Gas 6. Arrange the salmon in a baking dish. Season with pepper and bake in the oven for about 9 minutes, until just cooked through.

Meanwhile, cook the mangetout in boiling water for 3 minutes, then drain and refresh under cold water. Drain well and set aside.

Divide the salad leaves between four serving plates, scatter over the peppers, tomatoes, cucumber and mangetout. Make a dressing by whisking together the mint, lemon juice and rind and olive oil in a bowl. Season with salt and pepper to taste. Place a hot salmon fillet on each salad, drizzle over the dressing and serve.

**NOTES**

# Summer leaf, mozzarella and basil salad

**SERVES 4**

115g/4oz mixed summer leaves,
such as lollo rosso, cos and
lamb's lettuce
350g/12oz cherry tomatoes, halved
2 balls mozzarella cheese, torn into
bite-size chunks
2 avocados

**FOR THE DRESSING**

handful of fresh basil leaves
2 tsp capers, rinsed
1 tsp Dijon mustard
pinch of sugar
1 tbsp red-wine vinegar
4 tbsp olive oil
salt and freshly ground black pepper

First make the dressing. Put the basil, capers, mustard, sugar, vinegar and oil in a blender and process until smooth. Season to taste with salt and pepper and set aside. (The capers are already salty, so you may not need to add any extra salt.)

Divide the leaves among four individual serving bowls and scatter the tomatoes and mozzarella on top.

Halve the avocados, remove the stones, then peel and cut the flesh into bite-size chunks. Scatter over the salads.

Drizzle the dressing over the top of each serving, toss to combine well and serve immediately.

# Summer leaves with lemon and chilli squid

**SERVES 4**

350g/12oz squid, cleaned
juice of 2 lemons
pinch of dried chilli flakes
115g/4oz mixed summer leaves,
such as little gem lettuce, oakleaf
and rocket
1 red pepper, diced
4 tomatoes, cut into eighths
½ cucumber, sliced
2 tbsp finely chopped fresh mint
leaves
pinch of sugar
½ tsp grated lemon rind
4 tbsp olive oil
salt

Prepare the squid by separating the tentacles from the body pouch, then cutting both into large bite-size pieces. Put in a bowl, pour over half the lemon juice, sprinkle with the dried chilli flakes and leave to marinate for at least 15 minutes.

Meanwhile, make the salad. Divide the salad leaves between four serving plates and scatter over the red pepper, tomatoes and cucumber. Make a dressing by whisking together the mint, sugar, remaining lemon juice, lemon rind and 3 tablespoons of the olive oil. Season to taste with salt and set aside.

Drain the squid and pat dry on kitchen paper. Brush with the remaining oil, then season well with salt. Heat a griddle pan or grill until very hot, then use to cook the squid for about 45 seconds on each side, until the flesh is opaque and tender. Scatter the squid over the salad servings, drizzle with the dressing and toss to combine. Serve.

# watercress

Wild watercress can be seen growing in summer streams, although the vivid green bunches that arrive on the greengrocers' shelves have been cultivated in special beds with piped running water and are available all year round. (You should avoid gathering and eating wild watercress, as it has usually been infiltrated by liver flukes – parasites that can cause severe damage to the liver, if ingested.)

The robust, peppery flavour of raw watercress is delicious in salads, or it may be shredded and added to cooked dishes at the last minute. Some people, however, find watercress too powerful on its own, and prefer it combined with blander ingredients or used more as a flavouring. The shredded leaves are excellent stirred into creamy mashed potato just before serving, or combined with milder lettuce leaves in a salad, in a similar manner to fresh herbs. Spread savoury scones with thick cream cheese and top with a sprig of watercress, or shred a handful of leaves and sprinkle over an omelette while it cooks.

Choose watercress with large dark leaves and avoid any that is withered, limp or slimy. If a recipe requires only the leaves, simply pluck them off the stems. For salads, part of the stem is often trimmed off, leaving the more tender upper part and juicy leaves.

## Watercress soup (opposite)

**SERVES 4**
25g/1oz butter
1 onion, chopped
225g/8oz potatoes, chopped
750ml/26fl oz/3 cups vegetable stock
175g/6oz watercress
250ml/9fl oz/1 cup milk
4 tbsp single cream
salt and freshly ground black pepper

Melt the butter in a pan, then add the onion and fry gently for about 5 minutes until soft. Add the potatoes, pour over the stock and leave to simmer for about 15 minutes until the potatoes are tender.

Meanwhile, remove the green leaves from the watercress and roughly chop the stalks. Add the stalks to the pan and cook for about 2 minutes, then stir in the leaves, reserving a few to garnish, and cook for about 1 minute more.

Pour the contents of the pan into a food processor or blender and process until smooth. Return to the pan, stir in the milk and bring to simmering point. Remove from the heat, stir in the cream and season to taste with salt and pepper. Serve immediately, garnished with the reserved watercress leaves.

**NOTES**

# peas

Juicy bright-green peas, fresh from their pods, are one of the joys of summer. Once they are picked, however, their sugars rapidly turn into starch and, as peas in their pods are so often days old when they reach the shops, 'fresh' peas may be less sweet than those that have been frozen within hours of picking. But when really fresh peas are available, they are truly wonderful. It is well worth growing your own and picking them just before cooking. Also, try the invariably sweet and delicate mangetout and sugar snap peas, both of which are eaten whole, pod and all.

All types of peas should be cooked very briefly by plunging into boiling water – never salted as this will toughen the skin – until just tender. Then quickly drain and toss with butter, seasoning and – for a really delicious crowning touch – a scattering of chopped fresh mint. Peas are also fabulous in salads: simply refresh them under cold water as soon as they have been drained and toss them in. Try also adding them to thick omelettes or tortillas, or to creamy risotto rice, as in the classic Italian *risi e bisi*, or mash and pile them on to garlic-rubbed toast, then top with twists of Parma ham. Summer peas make wonderful refreshing soups, too, and they are frequently used in Indian curries, while sugar snaps and mangetout, with their sugary tang and crispy texture, make a great addition to Asian-style stir-fries.

## Baked chilli salmon with smashed peas

**SERVES 4**

4 salmon fillets,
about 175g/6oz each, skinned
salt and freshly ground black pepper
juice of 1 lemon
¼ tsp dried chilli flakes
2 tbsp olive oil
4 shallots, chopped
500g/1lb 2oz shelled fresh
or frozen peas
125ml/4fl oz/½ cup white wine

Preheat the oven to 200ºC/400ºF/Gas 6. Arrange the salmon fillets in a single layer in a baking dish, season with salt, then sprinkle over the lemon juice and dried chilli flakes. Bake in the oven for about 9 minutes, until just cooked through.

Meanwhile, heat the oil in a frying pan, add the shallots and cook over a medium heat for about 3 minutes. Add the peas and wine and simmer for about 5 minutes until tender. Using a hand blender or potato masher, blend to make a coarse mash. Season to taste with salt and pepper and divide between four warm serving plates. Top each serving with a cooked salmon fillet and serve.

**NOTES**

# Summer pea and ham soup

**SERVES 4**
2 tbsp olive oil
2 onions, chopped
500g/1lb 2oz shelled fresh or frozen peas
1.2 litres/2¾ pints/4¾ cups vegetable stock
6 tbsp crème fraîche
handful of fresh mint, chopped, plus extra to garnish
salt and freshly ground black pepper
4 slices Parma ham, snipped into bite-size pieces

Heat the oil in a large pan, add the onions and fry gently for about 5 minutes, until soft. Add the peas and stock and bring to the boil. Lower the heat and leave to simmer gently for about 5 minutes.

Allow the pea, onion and stock mixture to cool slightly, then pour into a blender or food processor and process until smooth. Stir in the crème fraîche and chopped mint and season to taste with salt and pepper.

Heat through, then ladle into four warm serving bowls. Sprinkle over the ham and the fresh mint garnish and serve.

# Sugar snap and roast pepper salad

**SERVES 4**
4 red peppers
300g/10½oz sugar snap peas
2 tsp red-wine vinegar
4 tsp olive oil
handful of fresh mint, roughly chopped
salt and freshly ground black pepper

Preheat the oven to 200°C/400°F/Gas 6.

Place the peppers on a baking sheet and roast in the oven for about 1 hour, until the skins are wrinkled and well browned. Transfer to a bowl, cover with clear film and leave to cool for about 15 minutes.

When the peppers are cool enough to handle, peel off the skins, cut in half and discard the core and seeds. Slice the flesh into strips, place in a serving bowl and set aside.

Plunge the sugar snap peas into a pan of boiling water for about 3 minutes, until just tender but still crisp. Drain and refresh under cold running water. Drain again and add to the peppers.

Whisk together the vinegar, olive oil and mint, then season to taste with salt and pepper. Pour over the peppers and peas, toss to combine and serve.

**NOTES**

# Fragrant sugar snap stir-fry with prawns

**SERVES 4**

2 tbsp oyster sauce
2 tsp soy sauce
1 tsp sesame oil
1 tsp brown sugar
2 tbsp sunflower oil
1 red chilli, seeded and chopped
2 cloves garlic, finely chopped
5cm/2in piece fresh ginger, peeled
and grated
450g/1lb sugar snap peas or
mangetout
500g/1lb 2oz raw tiger prawns,
peeled and deveined
bunch of spring onions, sliced
large handful of fresh
basil, torn
rice or noodles, to serve

Put the oyster sauce, soy sauce, sesame oil and brown sugar in a small bowl and stir until the sugar has dissolved. Set aside.

Heat the sunflower oil in a wok or large frying pan, then add the chilli, garlic and ginger and stir-fry for about 30 seconds. Toss in the sugar snap peas and stir-fry for a further 1 minute.

Add the prawns and spring onions to the wok and stir-fry for about 2 minutes, until the prawns turn pink.

Pour over the oyster and soy sauce mixture and cook for about 30 seconds more. Serve immediately on a bed of rice or noodles, with the chopped basil sprinkled over the top.

# Green peas braised with lettuce and spring onions

**SERVES 4**

25g/1oz butter
bunch of spring onions, sliced
diagonally into 2.5cm/1in lengths
2 little gem lettuces, shredded
300g/10½oz shelled fresh
or frozen peas
4 sprigs of fresh mint
3 tbsp white wine
salt and freshly ground black pepper

Melt the butter in a pan. Add the spring onions and stir over a medium heat for about 1 minute. Add the lettuces and peas and stir to coat in the butter.

Add the mint sprigs and wine, stir, then cover tightly and leave to cook gently over a low heat for about 15 minutes, stirring occasionally, until the lettuces and peas are tender. Season to taste with salt and pepper and serve immediately.

# beans

Beans in their various incarnations are one of the great pleasures of the summer table. Sweet, juicy green beans, fresh-tasting runner beans and earthy broad beans all have their own merits and are wonderfully versatile. Remember, however, to choose the freshest you can find, as their flavour deteriorates very quickly after picking.

Green beans and runner beans are cooked in a similar way. Just trim off the tops and tails – and for runner beans, strip out the coarse strings and slice – and boil or steam until just tender. Then serve, simply tossed in butter and seasoned with black pepper, or make into a salad by refreshing under cold water and tossing with flaked almonds, finely sliced red onion and a few tablespoons of vinaigrette. Also try them chopped and tossed into soups and pasta or stewed with tomatoes and summer herbs.

Broad beans need to be removed from their pods before cooking and, on all but the very young beans, the thick grey-green skin should also be removed. Broad beans have a starchy texture, making them good for puréeing and blending into soups and dips. Their mild yet pervasive flavour stands out well in rich stews and other cooked dishes, too. They are, however, great when simply boiled or steamed and served as an accompaniment.

## three-bean salad with lemon and mint

Make a dressing by whisking together 4 teaspoons of red-wine vinegar, 2½ tablespoons of olive oil, the grated rind of ½ lemon, 1 teaspoon of Dijon mustard, a pinch of sugar and 1½ teaspoons of chopped fresh mint. Then season to taste with salt and freshly ground black pepper and set aside. Bring a large pan of water to the boil, toss in 200g/7oz of shelled broad beans, 200g/7oz of trimmed green beans and 200g/7oz of trimmed, sliced runner beans. Cook for about 3 minutes until just tender, then drain and refresh under cold water. Drain again and tip into a salad bowl. If liked, snip 3 grilled bacon rashers over the top, then pour over the dressing and toss to combine well. Leave to stand for at least 30 minutes before serving.

**NOTES**

# Broad bean purée with seared scallops

**SERVES 4**
2 tbsp olive oil
3 shallots, finely chopped
450g/1lb shelled broad beans
5 tbsp white wine
salt and freshly ground black pepper

**FOR THE SCALLOPS**
16-20 scallops, cleaned
½ clove garlic, finely chopped
1 red chilli, seeded and
finely chopped
juice and grated rind of 1 lime
1 tbsp olive oil
6 fresh mint leaves, shredded

Heat the oil in a pan. Add the shallots and gently fry over a medium-low heat for about 3 minutes. Add the beans, pour over the wine, cover and simmer over a low heat for about 6 minutes until tender. Put the beans and juices in a food processor or blender and process to make a smooth purée. Return to the pan and season to taste with salt and pepper. Set aside and keep warm.

Place the scallops in a large bowl. Whisk together the garlic, chilli and lime juice and zest, season with salt and pour over the scallops, turning them to coat well.

Heat the oil in a large frying pan. Add the scallops and cook for 1-2 minutes on each side, until lightly browned and just cooked. Serve immediately with the warm bean purée, spooning over any juices from the pan and sprinkling with the shredded mint leaves.

# Green beans roasted with tomatoes and herb-stuffed trout

**SERVES 4**
450g/1lb green beans, trimmed
450g/1lb cherry tomatoes
2 cloves garlic, thinly sliced
2 tbsp olive oil
salt and freshly ground black pepper
4 trout, about 400g/14oz each,
cleaned
1½ lemons
bunch of fresh thyme

Preheat the oven to 220°C/425°F/Gas 7. Put the beans and tomatoes in a large baking dish or roasting tin and sprinkle over the garlic. Drizzle with the oil, season with salt and pepper and toss to coat well.

Make several slashes in skin of each trout, then season all over with salt and pepper. Slice one of the lemons and stuff into the cavity of each fish with some sprigs of thyme, then squeeze a little juice from the lemon half over each fish.

Nestle the prepared fish in among the beans and tomatoes in the baking dish. Cook in the oven for about 15 minutes, until the trout are cooked through and the beans and tomatoes are tender. Serve.

**NOTES**

# okra

The okra plant is native to Africa and its long, ridged seed pods are widely used in the cooking of that continent, as well as in the cuisines of the Caribbean, India and the Mediterranean. Okra is usually stewed, although it may be fried or steamed before combining with other ingredients.

The seeds are coated in a slimy substance that is released into dishes containing chopped or sliced okra, giving them a somewhat gloopy consistency. This is relished by some and is often exploited as a deliberate characteristic of okra dishes. But if it is not to your taste, okra pods can simply be trimmed and cooked whole, so that the viscous liquid cannot ooze out. The end result will still capture the delicate but distinct flavour of okra and is truly delicious.

When buying, look for small, bright-green pods that are firm and slightly springy when squeezed. To prepare them, trim off the stem without revealing the seeds, then either leave whole or cut up as required in the recipe.

## Mediterranean okra and tomato casserole

**This simple Mediterranean-style dish, mildly spiced with coriander, is the perfect way to enjoy tender whole okra. Serve it hot, warm or at room temperature – as a vegetable accompaniment or as an appetizer, with chunks of crusty bread for mopping up the juices.**

**SERVES 4**

2 tbsp olive oil
1 onion, halved and sliced
2 cloves garlic, finely chopped
2 tsp ground coriander
600g/1lb 5oz ripe tomatoes, peeled, seeded and chopped
125ml/4fl oz/½ cup white wine
4 tbsp water
salt and freshly ground black pepper
450g/1lb okra, trimmed
large handful of fresh flat-leaf parsley, chopped

Heat the oil in a large pan. Add the onion and garlic and gently fry for about 5 minutes. Stir in the coriander, then add the tomatoes, wine and water. Season to taste with salt and pepper and stir. Add the okra and gently fold in.

Bring to the boil, reduce the heat, cover and leave to simmer gently for about 20 minutes, stirring occasionally, until the okra is tender. Check the seasoning and serve, with the chopped parsley sprinkled over the top.

**NOTES**

# Chicken and okra gumbo

**This spicy soupy stew is a classic of the Cajun kitchen. Here, the okra is sliced to release its viscous juices, giving the gumbo its distinctive, thick consistency.**

**SERVES 4**

2 tbsp olive oil
1 onion, chopped
2 cloves garlic, finely chopped
1½ tbsp plain flour
550ml/19fl oz/2¼ cups chicken stock
2 green peppers, chopped
250g/9oz okra, trimmed and cut into 1cm/½in slices
3 tomatoes, peeled, seeded and chopped
2 tbsp tomato purée
leaves from 3-4 sprigs of fresh thyme
1 tsp cayenne pepper
300g/10½oz cooked chicken, cut into bite-size pieces
150g/5½oz sweetcorn kernels
Tabasco sauce, to taste

Heat the oil in a large pan. Add the onion and garlic and fry gently for about 5 minutes. Stir in the flour and cook for a further minute.

Off the heat, gradually stir in the chicken stock, then add the green peppers, okra, tomatoes, tomato purée, thyme leaves and cayenne pepper. Bring to the boil, reduce the heat, cover and leave to simmer for about 45 minutes, stirring occasionally to stop the gumbo from catching on the base of the pan.

Stir in the chicken and sweetcorn and cook for a further 30 minutes, stirring occasionally. Add Tabasco sauce to taste. Serve in the traditional manner - ladled over rice.

## indian-spiced okra

In India, okra - often referred to as "ladies' fingers" - is a popular vegetable accompaniment. To prepare in the Indian manner, heat approximately 2 tablespoons of oil in a large pan, then add 2 chopped onions and fry gently for about 5 minutes. Toss in 2 crushed garlic cloves and a few teaspoons of grated fresh ginger and fry for a further 2 minutes, stirring. Then stir in ½ teaspoon each of chilli powder and ground turmeric and 1½ teaspoons each of ground coriander and ground cumin, followed by 4 tomatoes that have been peeled, seeded and chopped. Add 300g/10½oz of trimmed okra, season to taste with salt, cover and cook over a gentle heat for about 20 minutes, stirring from time to time, until the okra is tender. Check the seasoning and serve sprinkled with chopped fresh coriander or mint.

# broccoli

The name broccoli comes from the Italian word for "arm" or "shoot", which is a wonderful description of the appearance of the tiny unopened flowerheads clustered at the end of broccoli's fleshy stems. A member of the cabbage family, broccoli for some reason seems infinitely more sophisticated a vegetable than cabbage and has a milder flavour. The most commonly found broccoli is calabrese, with its fat, round, bluish-green heads. It is in season from summer into early autumn. Exotic-looking romanesco, with its elegant, pointed, lime-green heads – which would not look out of place in a bouquet of flowers – follows later.

Despite its many incarnations, the different varieties of broccoli taste very similar and can be cooked in the same way – steamed or boiled as a simple accompaniment, added to stir-fries, pies and tarts and salads, tossed with pasta or cooked in gratins. Frequently paired with cauliflower, broccoli also goes well with cheese and hollandaise sauces and chopped bacon.

The heads are often regarded as the main attraction when it comes to eating broccoli, but the juicy stems are as much of a pleasure, so do not just cut them off and discard them. As stems are usually covered in a thick coarse skin, it is a good idea to peel this off before cooking.

When buying, look for fresh, green specimens and avoid any that have soft or withered stems, yellowing heads or heads speckled with dark patches or spots. To prepare, wash well, break the heads into florets and peel and cut the stems into bite-size pieces. Then boil, steam or stir-fry until just tender. Avoid overcooking.

### stir-fried broccoli with ginger and garlic

Fresh, bright-green broccoli is perfect for stir-frying. Cut the stems and florets into bite-size pieces and set aside. Heat 2 tablespoons of sunflower oil in a wok, then toss in 2 crushed garlic cloves and about 2 teaspoons of grated fresh ginger and stir-fry for about 30 seconds. Add the prepared broccoli, followed by a pinch of dried chilli flakes, then toss over the heat for about 2 minutes. Sprinkle over 1-2 teaspoons of soy sauce and 1½ teaspoons of mirin and toss for a further minute. Serve immediately.

**NOTES**

# Orecchiette with broccoli and anchovies

**Traditionally, orecchiette – or "little ears" – are used in this southern Italian dish, but any short pasta such as penne or farfalle can be substituted.**

**SERVES 4**

300g/10½oz orecchiette or other short pasta
salt and freshly ground black pepper
900g/2lb broccoli, heads cut into florets and stems peeled and sliced
2 tbsp olive oil
1 onion, finely chopped
3 cloves garlic, finely chopped
50g/1¾oz can anchovies, drained and finely chopped
25g/1oz Parmesan cheese, grated

Cook the pasta in a large pan of boiling salted water, according to the instructions on the packet.

While the pasta is cooking, cook the broccoli in a separate pan of boiling salted water for about 5 minutes, or until just tender. Drain, reserving a little of the cooking water.

Heat the oil in another large pan, add the onion and garlic and fry gently for about 5 minutes, until soft. Add the broccoli and about 4 tablespoons of the reserved cooking water and gently crush with the back of a spoon. Stir in the anchovies, crushing them into the mixture, and season to taste with black pepper.

Toss the cooked pasta with the broccoli and anchovy mixture. Serve immediately sprinkled with the Parmesan.

# Broccoli and blue cheese tart with walnut pastry

**SERVES 6**

80g/2¾oz plain flour
40g/1½oz walnuts, chopped
salt and freshly ground black pepper
40g/1½oz butter, chilled and diced
about 1 tbsp cold water
300g/10½oz broccoli, heads cut into florets and stems peeled and sliced
2 tbsp olive oil
1 onion, finely chopped
4 eggs
6 tbsp crème fraîche
60g/2¼oz Gorgonzola or other blue cheese, cubed

Put the flour, walnuts and a pinch of salt in a food processor and process until the nuts are ground. Add the butter and process until the mixture resembles fine breadcrumbs. With the machine running, add just enough water for the mixture to come together to form a soft ball of pastry. Wrap in clear film and chill in the fridge for 30 minutes.

Meanwhile, steam the broccoli for 5 minutes, until just tender, then set aside. Heat the oil in a large pan, add the onion and cook for about 5 minutes. Toss in the broccoli, crush lightly with the back of a spoon, then set aside. Preheat the oven to 200°C/400°F/Gas 6.

Roll out the pastry to line a 20cm/8in tart tin. Cover with foil, scatter over some baking beans and bake in the oven for 10 minutes. Remove the foil and beans and cook for a further 5-10 minutes until the base is crisp. Beat together the eggs and crème fraîche in a bowl, season well with salt and pepper, then set aside.

Scatter the cheese over the base of the pastry case, top with the broccoli, then pour over the egg mixture. Bake for about 20 minutes until the filling is just set and golden. Serve warm or cold.

# peppers

An assortment of different peppers is available throughout the summer and well into the autumn. Most are either green, red, orange or yellow in colour, though they do come in other hues, including the more unusual purple-black variety. They range in shape from squat and round to long and tapered and they vary in flavour, too. Green peppers are in fact the same as red ones, but are picked before ripening, giving them a sharper, more savoury tang. Red peppers, along with the orange and yellow varieties, have a marked sweetness. Black peppers have a similar flavour to green ones and, as they turn green on cooking, are best used raw.

Crisp and juicy, raw peppers are delicious in salads. When cooked, they become succulent and tender and the sweeter-flavoured peppers become even sweeter. They can be grilled, roasted, sautéed, stewed and stuffed. They are a staple of Mediterranean cuisine – added to countless appetizers, sauces and stews, made into soup, scattered on pizzas and tossed with pasta.

Buy only peppers that are firm and glossy. Avoid any that are soft, wrinkled or blemished. Peppers are usually seeded before cooking. To do this, cut in half through the stem and gently pull the two sides apart, then strip away the seeds and pithy membrane, before chopping, slicing or stuffing, as desired. To prepare for stuffing whole, just cut around the stalk and gently wiggle it to pull out along with the core and seeds. Any loose seeds can then be shaken out and the white pith inside trimmed away using a long-bladed knife.

### roast peppers

Roasting sweet red, yellow or orange peppers until blackened all over intensifies their sweetness and depth of flavour and gives them a luscious soft texture.

Place the peppers on a baking sheet, then bake in an oven preheated to 230°C/450°F/Gas 8 until blackened. Transfer to a bowl and cover with clear film, then leave to stand for about 10 minutes.

When the peppers are cool enough to handle, peel off the skin and remove the stalk and seeds, then use the peppers as required. Don't rinse the peppers after roasting, as they will lose their intense, caramely, smoky flavour.

**NOTES**

# Roast pepper, tomato and mozzarella salad

**SERVES 4**

6 ripe medium tomatoes
8 canned anchovy fillets, drained and halved lengthways
2 red peppers, roasted (see page 86), peeled and seeded
2 yellow peppers, roasted (see page 86), peeled and seeded
2 balls of mozzarella cheese, about 250g/9oz in total
2 handfuls of fresh basil leaves
2 tbsp capers, rinsed and chopped
1 clove garlic, crushed
1 tbsp red-wine vinegar
4 tbsp olive oil
freshly ground black pepper
crusty French bread, to serve

Cut a cross in the skin at the base of each tomato, place in a heatproof bowl and pour over boiling water to cover. Leave to stand for about 30 seconds, then drain and peel. Halve the tomatoes, remove the tough core and scoop the seeds into a sieve placed over a bowl. Press the seeds with the back of a spoon to squeeze out the juice, then discard the seeds and reserve the juice.

Chop the tomatoes into bite-size pieces and place in a salad bowl with the anchovies. Cut the peppers and mozzarella into bite-size pieces and add to the tomatoes. Tear the basil leaves and scatter over the top.

Add the capers, garlic, vinegar and oil and a good grinding of black pepper to the reserved tomato juice and whisk together. Pour over the salad, toss to combine, then leave to stand for about 15 minutes. Serve with plenty of bread for mopping up the juices.

# Lamb steaks with sweet pepper relish

**SERVES 4**

4 lamb leg steaks, about 200g/7oz each
2 cloves garlic, finely chopped
2 tsp ground cumin
1 tsp paprika
juice of 1 lemon
3 tbsp olive oil
salt and freshly ground black pepper
2 red peppers, seeded and roughly chopped
1 tsp balsamic vinegar
2 tsp capers, rinsed
handful of fresh basil leaves

Place the lamb steaks in a large dish. Whisk together half the garlic with the cumin, paprika, lemon juice and 1 tablespoon of the olive oil, then season to taste with salt and pepper. Pour over the steaks, turning to coat, then cover and leave to marinate in the fridge for 1 hour.

To prepare the relish, heat the remaining oil in a frying pan. Add the remaining garlic and fry gently for about 1 minute. Add the red peppers and cook, stirring frequently, for about 20 minutes, until tender. Tip into a food processor or blender, add the vinegar and capers and process until smooth. Add the basil, pulse briefly to chop, then season to taste with salt and pepper. Set aside.

Preheat the grill to hot and use to cook the leg steaks for about 6 minutes on each side, or until cooked to your liking. Serve immediately with the warm relish.

# Pepperonata pizza with summer vegetables *(opposite)*

**This recipe makes two large pizzas, though, if you prefer, you can divide the dough into four pieces to make four smaller ones. The sweet red and yellow pepper sauce makes a wonderful base for the tender, juicy, chargrilled vegetables and melting mozzarella.**

**MAKES 2 LARGE PIZZAS**

400g/14oz strong white bread flour
2 x 7g/⅕oz sachets of easy-blend dried yeast
1 tsp salt
250ml/9fl oz/1 cup lukewarm water
2 tbsp olive oil, plus extra for brushing
2 cloves garlic, chopped
1 red pepper, seeded and cut lengthways into strips
1 yellow pepper, seeded and cut lengthways into strips
250ml/9fl oz/1 cup passata
salt and freshly ground black pepper
handful of fresh basil leaves
1 courgette, sliced into rounds
1 small aubergine, sliced into rounds
2 balls of mozzarella cheese, about 125g/4½oz each, diced
handful of black olives (optional)

Combine the flour, yeast and salt in a large bowl and make a well in the centre. Pour the water into the well and gradually work the flour mixture into it to make a soft, non-sticky dough. Turn out on to a lightly floured surface and knead for 5-10 minutes until the dough becomes smooth and elastic. Place in a lightly oiled bowl, cover in clear film and leave to rise in a warm place for about 45 minutes, until doubled in size.

Meanwhile, prepare the pepperonata sauce and chargrilled vegetables. Heat the oil in a large pan, add the garlic and fry gently for about 2 minutes, then add the peppers and cook gently for a further 5 minutes. Add the passata, season to taste with salt and pepper, cover and simmer for about 25 minutes, stirring occasionally, particularly towards the end of the cooking time. Remove from the heat, tear half the basil leaves into the sauce, check the seasoning, then set aside.

While the sauce is simmering, preheat the oven to 220°C/425°C/Gas 7. Heat a ridged griddle pan or grill until hot. Brush the aubergine and courgette slices on both sides with a little olive oil and season with salt and pepper, then, working in batches, cook on the hot griddle or grill for about 3 minutes on each side until charred and tender. Set aside.

On a lightly floured surface, punch down the dough and divide into two pieces. Press each one flat and roll out to form two 25cm/10in-diameter rounds.

Spread the pepperonata sauce over the rounds of dough and arrange the cooked vegetables and mozzarella on top. Scatter over the olives, if using, and bake in the oven for 15-20 minutes, until the cheese is bubbling and the crust golden. Grind over black pepper, sprinkle with the remaining basil leaves and serve.

**NOTES**

# tomatoes

Ripened in the hot summer sunshine, tomatoes should be juicy, sweet and intensely flavoured and equally good whether they are eaten raw or cooked. In season well into autumn, they are used across the globe as a base for sauces, stews, soups and salads. They can even be made into ice creams and sorbets. They come in a fabulous array of shapes, sizes and colours – round or plum-shaped, smooth or ridged, huge or tiny, and in various shades of red, orange, yellow or green.

When buying tomatoes, choose those that are deeply coloured and unblemished. They take little preparation, although some recipes may call for them to be peeled and seeded. To peel, cut a cross in the skin at the base of each tomato and place in a heatproof bowl. Pour over boiling water and leave to stand for about 30 seconds, then drain. The skins should peel away easily. To remove the seeds, slice in half, cut out the core and gently press out the seeds with your thumb. A fragrant sauce can be made by gently frying 2 crushed garlic cloves in 2 tablespoons of olive oil for 1–2 minutes, then adding 675g/1½lb of tomatoes that have been peeled, seeded and chopped. Simmer gently for about 15 minutes and season to taste with salt and freshly ground black pepper. Remove from the heat, stir in a handful of torn fresh basil leaves and use.

## Oven-dried tomatoes on garlic bruschetta

**MAKES 12**
450g/1lb cherry tomatoes, halved
2 cloves garlic, finely chopped
3 tbsp olive oil
salt and freshly ground black pepper

**FOR THE BRUSCHETTA**
12 slices baguette or ciabatta, 1.5cm/¾in thick
1 clove garlic, halved
handful of fresh basil leaves
extra virgin olive oil, for drizzling

Preheat the oven to 170°C/325°F/Gas 3. Arrange the tomatoes, cut-side up, in a baking dish. Mix the garlic and olive oil in a small bowl, season to taste with salt and pepper, and spoon the mixture over the tomatoes. Bake in the oven for 1–1¼ hours, until the tomatoes are slightly shrivelled but still red. Remove from the oven and leave to cool.

To make the bruschetta, grill the bread on both sides until golden, then rub one side of each slice with the cut garlic clove. Top with tomato halves, spooning over any juices, add a couple of basil leaves, then drizzle with oil and serve.

**NOTES**

# Gazpacho

**SERVES 4**

900g/2lb ripe tomatoes, peeled (see page 90), seeded and chopped
½ cucumber, peeled and chopped
1 red pepper, seeded and chopped
2 cloves garlic, chopped
2 tbsp sherry vinegar
4 tbsp olive oil
3 slices white bread, crusts removed
400ml/14fl oz/1⅔ cups cold water
salt and freshly ground black pepper
croûtons and fresh basil leaves, to serve

Put the tomatoes, cucumber, red pepper, garlic, vinegar and olive oil in a blender or food processor. Tear up the bread into small chunks and sprinkle over the top, then pour over about half the water. Process to make a smooth purée.

Pour the purée into a large bowl, stir in the remaining water and season to taste with salt and pepper. Cover and leave to chill in the fridge for at least 2 hours.

Serve with croûtons and roughly torn fresh basil leaves sprinkled over each serving.

# Baked chicken with cinnamon and honey-roast tomatoes

**SERVES 4**

4 skinless chicken breasts, about 200g/7oz each
1 clove garlic, crushed
1 tsp smoked paprika
juice of 1 lemon
2 tbsp olive oil
salt and freshly ground black pepper
8 ripe medium tomatoes, halved
1 tsp ground cinnamon
2-3 tsp runny honey

Arrange the chicken breasts in a single layer in a baking dish. In a small bowl, whisk together the garlic, paprika, lemon juice and half the olive oil. Season to taste with salt and pepper, then pour over the chicken breasts and turn to coat well. Cover and leave to marinate in the fridge for at least 1 hour.

Preheat the oven to 220°C/425°F/Gas 7. Tuck in the tomatoes, cut-side up, around the chicken breasts. Sprinkle over the cinnamon, season well with salt and pepper, then drizzle the honey and the remaining olive oil on top.

Bake in the oven for about 25 minutes, spooning the juices over once or twice during the cooking time, until the tomatoes are tender and the chicken cooked through. Serve.

# Tomato, red pepper and ricotta tartlets

**SERVES 4**

2 large red peppers, roasted (see page 86), peeled and seeded
150g/5½oz cherry tomatoes
1 tsp balsamic vinegar
100g/3/½oz ricotta cheese
salt and freshly ground black pepper
olive oil, for drizzling
few fresh basil leaves, to serve

**FOR THE PASTRY**

40g/1½oz walnuts
115g/4oz wholemeal flour
pinch of salt
55g/2oz butter, chilled and diced
about 1 tbsp cold water

First make the pastry. Put the walnuts in a food processor and process until ground. Add the flour and salt and pulse to combine. Add the butter and process until the mixture resembles fine breadcrumbs. With the motor running, gradually add just enough cold water for the mixture to come together and form a ball. Wrap in clear film and chill in the fridge for about 30 minutes.

Preheat the oven to 190°C/375°F/Gas 5. Roll out the pastry and use to line four greased 10cm/4in-diameter tart tins. Cover each with foil, fill with baking beans and bake in the oven for 8 minutes. Remove the foil and beans, then bake for a further 4 minutes until the bases are dry. Remove from the oven and reduce the temperature to 180°C/350°F/Gas 4.

Meanwhile, cut the peppers into strips. Halve the tomatoes. Divide the pepper strips between the baked tart cases, then tuck the tomatoes in amongst them. Drizzle with balsamic vinegar and top with a large spoonful of ricotta. Season to taste with salt and pepper and bake in the oven for about 20 minutes. Serve hot or cold, drizzled with olive oil and scattered with fresh basil.

# Meatballs in tomato sauce

**SERVES 4**

350g/12oz minced lean beef
1 onion, grated
1 clove garlic, crushed
2 tsp finely chopped fresh thyme
2 tbsp grated Parmesan cheese
salt and freshly ground black pepper
1 tbsp olive oil
450g/1lb tomatoes, peeled (see page 90), seeded and chopped
6 sun-dried tomatoes in oil, drained and sliced
spaghetti, to serve

In a large bowl, combine the beef, onion, garlic, half the thyme and the Parmesan cheese and season well with salt and pepper. Roll the mixture into 35–40 bite-size balls. Place on a plate, cover and leave to chill in the fridge for at least 30 minutes.

Heat the oil in a large frying pan until hot, then add the meatballs and cook over a medium-high heat until they are browned all over. Work in batches if necessary.

Return all the meatballs to the pan. Add the fresh and sun-dried tomatoes and the remaining thyme, season to taste with salt and pepper, lower the heat and leave to simmer gently for about 20 minutes, until the meatballs are cooked through and tender. Serve with spaghetti.

**NOTES**

# aubergines

A central ingredient in the Mediterranean kitchen, the aubergine is actually a native of Asia and holds a prominent place in that continent's cuisine as well. In season from midsummer through into autumn, they thrive in warm, sunny climates, although they can be grown in cooler regions too. There are many different varieties, coming in a vast array of shapes, sizes and colours. Plump, glossy, purple-black aubergines may be large or small enough to be eaten in two or three mouthfuls. Then there are the lavender-purple, green and creamy-white varieties, some long and thin, others fat and round or small and egg-shaped. And, in addition, there are also the tiny hard oriental aubergines, barely the size of a large pea, that are frequently used in Thai curries and that explode tantalizingly in your mouth as you bite into them.

Aubergines are delicious stewed in dishes such as French *ratatouille* and Indian and Thai curries, baked as in Greek *moussaka* and Italian *parmigiana di melanzane*, or simply sliced, dipped in batter and deep-fried. They become tender and juicy with an almost meaty texture when cooked and readily absorb the flavours of the other ingredients they are with.

When buying, look for firm, shiny specimens and avoid any that are soft or wrinkled. Size makes little difference to flavour and texture, so choose aubergines that are appropriate to the recipe. The larger ones, for example, are great for stuffing and the smallest ones are ideal for using whole in curries and stew.

## simple aubergine dip

The soft flesh of baked aubergines is used throughout the Mediterranean and Middle East to make a delicious dip for serving as an appetizer, a side dish or part of a *mezze*. Simply take 2 large aubergines, prick them with a fork and bake in a preheated oven at 200°C/400°F/Gas 6 for about 30–40 minutes, until soft. Scoop out the creamy flesh into a blender or food processor and discard the skins. Add 2 chopped garlic cloves, ½ a sliced onion, the juice of 1 lemon and a handful of roughly chopped fresh flat-leaf parsley. Process until smooth. Season to taste with salt and freshly ground black pepper and serve with more chopped parsley sprinkled over.

**NOTES**

# Melting aubergine and Parmesan rolls

**In this twist on the classic *parmigiana di melanzane*, the aubergines are sliced lengthways and rolled around tomatoes and melting mozzarella.**

**SERVES 4**

2 tbsp olive oil, plus extra
for brushing
2 cloves garlic, finely chopped
675g/1½lb ripe tomatoes, peeled
(see page 90) and coarsely
chopped
salt and freshly ground black pepper
large handful of fresh basil leaves
2 aubergines, cut lengthways into
2mm/⅛in thick slices
1 ball of mozzarella cheese, about
150g/5½oz, diced
55g/2oz Parmesan cheese, grated

Preheat the oven to 200°C/400°F/Gas 6. Grease a large baking dish thoroughly.

Heat the oil in a pan, add the garlic and fry gently for 1–2 minutes. Add the tomatoes, season with salt and pepper, lower the heat and leave to simmer for about 15 minutes, until you have a thick sauce. Remove from the heat, tear half the basil leaves into the sauce, check the seasoning and set aside.

Meanwhile, heat a ridged griddle pan or grill until hot. Brush the aubergine slices lightly with oil on both sides. Season with salt and pepper and, working in batches, cook on the griddle or under the grill for about 3 minutes on each side, until charred and tender. Roll up and keep the cooked slices warm while cooking the rest.

Drizzle a spoonful of tomato sauce in the centre of each cooked aubergine slice, sprinkle over a few cubes of mozzarella and a little Parmesan, then top with a little more sauce. Roll up and place in the baking dish, folded side down. Sprinkle over the remaining Parmesan, grind over a little black pepper and bake in the oven for about 15 minutes until tender and golden. Serve sprinkled with the remaining basil leaves.

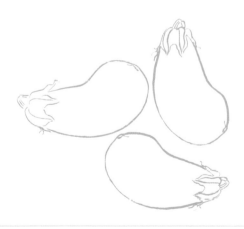

# Warm aubergine salad with herb salsa (opposite)

**SERVES 4**
½ clove garlic
large handful of fresh basil leaves,
plus extra to garnish
5 tbsp olive oil, plus extra for
brushing
1 tbsp balsamic vinegar
2 tbsp capers, rinsed
salt and freshly ground black pepper
1 tbsp pinenuts
2 large aubergines

Make a dressing by putting the garlic, basil, olive oil, vinegar and capers in a food processor or blender. Process until smooth, season to taste with salt and pepper and set aside.

Heat a dry frying pan, add the pinenuts and toss over the heat for about 3 minutes until golden. Remove from the pan and set aside.

Slice the aubergines lengthways into 5mm/¼in-thick slices and brush on both sides with olive oil, then season with salt and pepper. Heat a ridged griddle pan or grill until hot, then, working in batches, use to cook the aubergine slices for about 3 minutes on each side, until charred and tender. Roll up and keep the cooked slices warm while cooking the rest.

Divide the cooked aubergine slices among four serving plates, drizzle over the dressing, sprinkle over the toasted pinenuts and serve, scattered with a few fresh basil leaves.

# Sicilian aubergine salad

**SERVES 4**
3 tbsp olive oil
2 cloves garlic, thinly sliced
1 onion, halved and thinly sliced
1 aubergine, cut into 1cm/½in cubes
1 tbsp tomato purée
8 tbsp vegetable stock
3 ripe tomatoes, peeled (see
page 90) and chopped
1 tsp red-wine vinegar
2 tsp sugar
2 tbsp capers, rinsed
handful of green olives, stoned
freshly ground black pepper
large handful of fresh flat-leaf
parsley, roughly chopped

Heat the oil in a large frying pan, add the garlic and onion and gently fry for about 5 minutes. Toss in the aubergine and cook for a further 10 minutes, stirring occasionally.

Blend the tomato purée and stock together in a clean pan, then add to the aubergines with the tomatoes, vinegar, sugar, capers and olives and season to taste with black pepper. Bring to the boil, then lower the heat and leave to simmer for about 15 minutes, stirring occasionally, until the aubergine is tender. Check the seasoning and adjust if necessary.

Transfer to a bowl and leave to stand for at least 30 minutes. Serve at room temperature, sprinkled with the chopped parsley.

**NOTES**

# cucumbers

Made up almost entirely of water, the juicy, refreshing cucumber comes in many shapes and sizes, from tiny, knobbly specimens to long, plump, smooth-skinned ones – and, although they are subtle, there are distinct shifts of flavour between the different varieties.

Cucumbers are used the world over, especially in salads and relishes, their mild flavour often being used to carry stronger flavourings or to provide a calming accompaniment to fiercer seasonings, such as chillies and spices. They are frequently paired with yoghurt, soured cream and cheese – a tradition that spreads from the eastern Mediterranean right through the Middle East and into India. Chopped cucumber is a central ingredient of *raita*, a cooling, minty yoghurt relish for serving alongside spicy curries, while in Greece it is stirred with yoghurt and mint to make the dip *tzatziki*, and the similar *cacik* in Turkey and other parts of the Middle East. It is also popular pickled or marinated with herbs, vinegar and spices – a tradition particularly associated with central and eastern Europe.

When buying, look for firm cucumbers. Although the skin is edible, it can easily be removed using a vegetable peeler, if desired. You can also quickly remove the seeds by halving the cucumber lengthways and scooping them out with a teaspoon. The flesh may then be sliced, diced, grated or cut into batons, ready to add to any dish you choose.

### tzatziki

Peel, seed and grate 1 small or ½ a large cucumber into a strainer and press out as much liquid as possible. Tip the remaining flesh into a bowl and combine with 240ml/8fl oz/scant 1 cup of Greek yoghurt, 1 crushed clove garlic and 2 tablespoons of chopped fresh mint. Stir in salt to taste, then chill in the fridge until ready to serve.

**NOTES**

# Cucumber and mango salad

Crunchy, refreshing cucumber is perfect for adding to any summer salad. Its mild taste and crispness provide a great foundation upon which to build other flavours, textures and colours to create a really zingy and interesting dish. The juicy summer fruits used here are excellent combined with the crisp vegetables - their sweetness offsetting and enhancing both the flavour of the vegetables and the tartness of the vinegar. Although the recipe given below uses mangoes or peaches, other seasonal fruits can be substituted, according to availability. Good alternatives might include a few of handfuls of blueberries or strawberries, or perhaps some pitted cherries. But whatever fruit you decide to use, always make sure that it is really ripe and bursting with flavour.

**SERVES 4**
1 cucumber, seeded and diced
1 tomato, seeded and diced
2 green peppers, seeded and diced
2 small mangoes or 2 large peaches,
stoned, peeled and diced
salt and freshly ground black pepper
1½ tbsp red-wine vinegar
2 tbsp olive oil

Put the cucumber, tomato, green peppers and mangoes or peaches in a large serving bowl and season to taste with salt and pepper.

Whisk together the red-wine vinegar and olive oil in a small bowl to make a simple dressing. Drizzle this over the vegetables and fruit, toss to combine thoroughly and serve.

## marinated cucumber

This simple sweet-and-sour dish, scented with fragrant dill, makes a good accompaniment to cold meats and grilled fish.

Thinly slice a large cucumber into a colander, sprinkle with a generous pinch of salt, tossing to coat, then leave to drain for about 30 minutes. Meanwhile, heat a dry frying pan and use to toast 1 teaspoon of coriander seeds. Lightly crush them in a mortar, then combine with 2 tablespoons of white-wine vinegar and 1 teaspoon of sugar. Squeeze out as much liquid from the cucumber as possible, place in a bowl, sprinkle with a large handful of finely chopped fresh dill and pour over the vinegar mixture. Toss to coat and chill for at least 1 hour before serving.

**NOTES**

# summer squashes

Available from midsummer and through into the autumn, summer squashes – usually distinguishable from the winter varieties by their thin edible skin – come in a wide range of shapes and sizes, often with skins in vibrant eye-catching hues of green, yellow or orange. Dark-green and bright-yellow courgettes are probably the most readily available, but bulb-bottomed crooknecks with their curved stems, tiny fying-saucer-shaped pattypans and giant marrows are all part of the same family, and well worth looking out for. Marrows can grow to an enormous size, but are best eaten when still fairly small. They are, in fact, just large courgettes.

All summer squashes are delicately flavoured and have tender juicy flesh when cooked. Really small and tender courgettes, pattypans and crooknecks can be cooked whole, if wished, then simply tossed in butter and seasoned, but larger squashes should be topped and tailed, then sliced, chopped or grated before using. They may be boiled, sautéed or grilled. Marrows tend to have a toughish skin, so should also be peeled. They can be halved lengthways and have their seeds scooped out, to create the perfect vehicle for stuffing and baking. Courgettes, crooknecks and pattypans are all delicious served hot or cold in salads, pasta dishes and tarts, and also make a good addition to summer vegetable stews and sauces.

When buying summer squashes, remember to select only the firm, glossy specimens. Avoid any that are limp and dull-looking or have soft patches.

### deep-fried courgette flowers

Courgette flowers are available in late spring and early summer. They can be added to salads and pasta dishes and make a delicious appetizer when deep-fried. To prepare, whisk together 115g/4oz flour, 170ml/5½fl oz/generous ⅔ cup light Italian beer and a pinch of salt to make a smooth batter. In a separate bowl, whisk 1 egg white until stiff, then fold it into the batter. Fill a large pan about two-thirds full with vegetable oil and heat until just starting to smoke (about 190°C/375°F). Working in batches of 4–5 flowerheads at a time, dip them in the batter, then drop into the hot oil and cook for 2–3 minutes until crisp and golden. Lift out using a slotted spoon and drain on kitchen paper. Serve, sprinkled with salt.

**NOTES**

# Chargrilled courgette and feta salad

Summer

**SERVES 4**

2 tbsp chopped fresh mint leaves
juice and grated rind of ½ lemon
pinch of sugar
3 tbsp olive oil, plus extra for brushing
salt and freshly ground black pepper
4 courgettes, cut diagonally into 5mm/¼in thick slices
175g/6oz feta cheese

Make a dressing by putting the mint, lemon juice and rind, sugar and olive oil in a bowl and seasoning with a little salt and plenty of pepper. Whisk until well blended and set aside.

Brush the courgette slices with a little oil. Heat a griddle pan or grill until hot and use to cook the courgettes for about 2–3 minutes on each side, until just tender. (You will probably need to work in batches.)

Put the hot courgettes in a large serving bowl, crumble over the feta cheese, pour over the dressing, toss to combine and serve either warm or at room temperature.

# Spaghetti with courgettes and capers

**SERVES 4**

2 tbsp olive oil
1 onion, finely chopped
2 cloves garlic, finely chopped
4 courgettes, grated
1 tbsp capers, rinsed and chopped, plus 1½ tbsp whole capers, rinsed
300g/10½oz spaghetti
salt and freshly ground black pepper
85g/3oz Parmesan cheese, grated

Heat the olive oil in a large pan. Add the onion and garlic and fry gently for about 5 minutes, then add the courgettes and chopped capers and cook, stirring, for about 10 minutes until the courgettes are tender. Leave in the pan and set aside.

Meanwhile, cook the pasta in boiling salted water according to the instructions on the packet. Drain well.

Stir the whole capers into the courgette mixture and season well with black pepper and a little salt if necessary. (The capers are salty, so you probably will not need to add any extra salt.) Add the spaghetti and toss to coat, then sprinkle over two-thirds of the Parmesan cheese and toss again. Serve, sprinkled with the remaining cheese.

NOTES

# Summer vegetable and tuna kebabs

**SERVES 4**

1½ cloves garlic, crushed
¼ tsp roughly chopped fresh oregano leaves
3 tbsp olive oil
salt and freshly ground black pepper
1 red onion, seeded and cut into eighths
2 courgettes, sliced
450g/1lb cherry tomatoes
1 red pepper, seeded and cut into chunks
600g/1lb 5oz fresh tuna, cubed

Preheat the grill to hot or prepare the barbecue.

In a small bowl, make a marinade by whisking together the garlic, oregano and olive oil. Season well with salt and pepper and set aside.

Thread alternate pieces of vegetables and fish on to twelve kebab skewers. Lay in a single layer in a large dish and pour over the marinade, turning to coat well.

Cook the kebabs on the grill or barbecue for about 8 minutes, until the vegetables are just tender and the fish cooked through, turning the skewers during cooking.

# Spiced marrow

**With its mild, juicy flavour, marrow goes well with pungent Indian spices, making a light yet zesty dish. Serve as a vegetable accompaniment or as part of a meal with a varied selection of curries, accompanied by fragrant pilau rice and flatbreads.**

**SERVES 4**

2 tbsp tomato purée
250ml/9fl oz/1 cup water
2 tbsp sunflower oil
1 onion, halved and sliced
2 cloves garlic, sliced
2 green chillies, seeded and sliced
5cm/2in piece fresh ginger, peeled and grated
1 tsp ground coriander
½ tsp ground turmeric
1 small marrow, peeled, seeded and cut into chunks
salt
juice of ½ lemon
large handful of fresh coriander, roughly chopped

Blend the tomato purée with about a quarter of the water in a small bowl, then set aside. Heat the oil in a large pan, add the onion and garlic and fry for about 5 minutes, until soft. Add the chillies and ginger and fry for a further minute.

Stir in the ground coriander and turmeric, then pour in the tomato purée and water mixture. Add the marrow chunks, turning to coat in the sauce, then season to taste with salt and bring to the boil. Reduce the heat, cover and leave to simmer gently for about 10 minutes, stirring occasionally.

Uncover the pan and cook for a further 5 minutes, until the marrow is tender. Check the seasoning, stir in the lemon juice and serve, with the chopped fresh coriander sprinkled over the top.

# sweetcorn

Like peas, corn is best eaten as soon as possible after picking, as the sugars start to turn rapidly to starch when the cobs have been harvested. A type of maize, sweetcorn is a summer treat that stretches into early autumn. Whole cobs can be boiled or barbecued until tender, then eaten whole, drenched in butter and seasoned with salt and freshly ground black pepper - a truly wonderful experience, as the sweet juicy kernels explode in your mouth and mingle with the spicy pepper and lush creamy butter.

The kernels can also be stripped off the cob and used in numerous dishes. They are a great addition to the delicious cornbreads and corn puddings of the southern United States, and are no less out of place in corn fritters, creamy chowders, spicy curries or light refreshing salads.

Baby corncobs - just a few centimetres long - are immature cobs, picked before they are fully grown. They can be eaten whole, either raw or lightly cooked, in salads or served with dips. They are also fabulous tossed into stir-fries.

Buy the freshest corn possible, preferably still in its green husks, which must be stripped off, along with the silky threads underneath, before cooking. Then simply cook in a pan of boiling water for 5-10 minutes, until the kernels are tender. If just the kernels are required, hold the cob upright on a board and, with a sharp knife, strip them away from the cob with a downward motion.

## roast corn with chilli butter

Barbecued corncobs are one of the great pleasures of summer and are especially good served with zesty chilli and lime butter.

First prepare the butter, by beating together 55g/2oz of softened butter with 1 finely chopped, seeded red chilli and the grated rind of 1½ limes. Shape into a log, wrap in clear film and leave to chill in the fridge for at least 30 minutes to firm up.

Meanwhile, soak the unhusked corncobs in cold water for 15 minutes. Drain well, then roast on a rack over the glowing coals of a barbecue for 15-20 minutes, turning from time to time, until they are cooked on all sides and the kernels are tender. To serve, pull away the husks and silky threads and enjoy dotted with the chilli butter.

**NOTES**

# Sweetcorn chowder

**SERVES 4**

2 tbsp olive oil
1 onion, chopped
2 cloves garlic, chopped
2 red chillies, seeded and chopped
kernels from 4 corncobs, about
500g/1lb 2oz in weight
300g/10½oz potatoes, diced
825ml/30fl oz/3⅓ cups vegetable or
chicken stock
400ml/14fl oz/1⅔ cups milk
4 tbsp double cream
handful of fresh flat-leaf parsley,
chopped
salt and freshly ground black pepper

Heat the oil in a pan, then add the onion and garlic and fry gently for about 5 minutes. Stir in the chillies and cook for 1-2 minutes, then add the corn kernels, potatoes and stock. Bring to the boil, reduce the heat and leave to simmer for 10-15 minutes, until the corn and potatoes are tender.

Transfer about a quarter of the soup to a food processor or blender and process until smooth. Pour back into the pan and stir to combine well.

Add the milk and heat gently until almost at a simmer. Remove from the heat, stir in the cream and chopped parsley, season to taste with salt and pepper and serve.

# Corn salad with chilli, peppers, herbs and smoked trout

**SERVES 4**

1 green chilli, seeded and
finely chopped
grated rind and juice of 1 lime
2 tbsp sunflower oil
salt
4 corncobs
1 red pepper, seeded and diced
3 smoked trout fillets, about
175g/6oz each
large handful of fresh coriander,
roughly chopped

First make the dressing. Whisk together the chilli, lime rind and juice, oil and a pinch of salt in a small bowl. Set aside.

Bring a pan of water to the boil. Strip the husks and silky threads from the corncobs and add them to the pan. Return to the boil, then lower the heat and leave to simmer for 5-10 minutes until the kernels are tender. Drain, refresh under cold water and pat dry.

Hold each cob upright on a board and, using a sharp knife, slice downwards to remove the kernels. Discard the cobs.

Put the kernels in a bowl with the red pepper and flake the trout fillets on top. Sprinkle over the chopped coriander, then pour over the dressing and toss lightly to combine. Serve.

# shallots

Shallots are a member of the onion family. In season well into autumn, they are much smaller than most varieties of onion and also have a more potent flavour. The four most common varieties are the long, torpedo-shaped banana shallots, the pungent pink shallots with their reddish skin and pinky flesh, the mild brown shallots that tend to be divided into separate bulbs inside the skin, and the pungent, red Asian shallots that are often pounded into curry pastes along with other spices.

Like onions, shallots are frequently used to add an extra tang to sauces, stews and dressings, but they can also be enjoyed as an ingredient in their own right. Try them pickled, caramelized, roasted or used as a tart filling. Their intense flavour makes them useful for adding to sauces where you want extra flavour, without the bulk that would come from using onions.

## Roast shallot, tomato and thyme salad (opposite)

**SERVES 4**
2 tbsp olive oil
1 tbsp balsamic vinegar
1 tsp soft brown sugar
350g/12oz shallots, peeled
salt and freshly ground black pepper
350g/12oz cherry tomatoes, halved
2 large handfuls of rocket and watercress leaves
15g/½oz Parmesan cheese, shaved

**FOR THE DRESSING**
leaves from a few sprigs of fresh thyme
½ clove garlic, crushed
½ tbsp red-wine vinegar
4 tsp olive oil

Preheat the oven to 200°C/400°F/Gas 6. In a small bowl, whisk together the olive oil, balsamic vinegar and sugar. Put the shallots in a baking dish, then drizzle over the oil and vinegar mixture and toss to coat. Season with salt and pepper and roast in the oven for about 30 minutes, shaking the dish once or twice during the cooking time, until tender and browned.

Meanwhile, prepare the dressing. Gently bruise the thyme leaves in a mortar, then add the garlic, red-wine vinegar and olive oil and whisk together. Season with salt and pepper and set aside.

Put the tomatoes and roasted shallots in a bowl. Drizzle with the dressing and toss to combine. Divide the rocket and watercress leaves among four serving plates, spoon the tomatoes and shallots on top and scatter with the Parmesan shavings. Serve immediately.

NOTES

# beetroot

Dark-purple beetroot with its rich, magenta juice and sweet flavour is available for most of the year – either in season in summer and autumn, or from the cold-store throughout the winter. Beetroot ranges from tiny globes to roots the size of a fist, its fat, rounded shape narrowing to a delicate point at the whispy root-end. Buy it with the delicate, pink-tinged green leaves still attached, if you can, as these can be used like spinach or added to salads.

Beetroot is wonderfully versatile. It makes a good vegetable in its own right and is excellent puréed to create a warming, hearty soup, or even an elegant, chilled one. It can also be chopped and tossed into stews and roasted or baked with other roots until sweet and juicy. The mild, sweet flavour makes a good foil for any sharp, salty ingredients in a dish and the juice will leach out, giving an attractive reddish-purple hue. For a delicious, eye-catching salad, try pairing beetroot with juicy orange segments, slices of red onion and a sprinkling of zesty mint, or go for an East European touch by mixing it with pickled herrings, soured cream and fresh dill.

When buying, look for firm, undamaged specimens, and try to buy roots of an even size for ease of cooking. Twist off the leaves and wash gently under the tap. Then boil or bake in a moderate oven until tender. The skin will slip off easily after cooking and should be discarded.

### baked beetroot
One of the simplest ways to cook beetroot is to bake it in a lightly spiced olive-oil dressing until sweet and tender. Trim and peel 6 medium-sized roots, then cut into quarters – or wedges, if large – and put in a baking dish. Whisk together 1 tablespoon of balsamic vinegar, 2 tablespoons of olive oil, 1 teaspoon of ground cumin and 1 finely chopped clove of garlic, then season with salt and freshly ground black pepper. Pour this mixture over the beetroot, then toss to coat. Bake in a preheated oven at 200°C/400°F/Gas 6 for about 40 minutes, turning once or twice during cooking, until tender. Serve hot, warm or cold, sprinkled with a handful of chopped fresh mint or parsley.

# Beetroot salad with grilled halloumi

**SERVES 4**

200g/7oz halloumi cheese, sliced
into 5-7mm/¼-⅓in-thick slices
1 red chilli, seeded and
finely chopped
1 clove garlic, crushed
juice of 1 lemon
3 tbsp olive oil
1 tbsp red-wine vinegar
pinch of sugar
grated rind of ½ lemon
1½ tsp chopped fresh mint leaves
salt and freshly ground black pepper
115g/4oz lamb's lettuce or other
summer leaves
300g/10½oz cooked beetroot, cut
into slim wedges

Arrange the halloumi in a dish in a single layer. Whisk together the chilli, garlic, lemon juice and 1 tablespoon of the oil in a small bowl and pour over the halloumi. Turn to coat well, then leave to marinate for at least 30 minutes.

Make a dressing by whisking together the vinegar, sugar, lemon rind, mint and remaining olive oil in a small bowl. Season to taste with salt and pepper and set aside. Preheat the grill to hot and line the grill pan with foil, or heat a ridged griddle pan.

Divide the lamb's lettuce or other salad leaves between four serving plates and scatter the beetroot wedges on top.

Place the halloumi slices on the prepared grill pan or griddle pan and cook on each side until lightly charred and just starting to bubble. Scatter the halloumi over the prepared salads. Drizzle with the dressing and serve immediately.

## beetroot and yoghurt dip

In the Middle East, beetroot and yoghurt are frequently paired. This healthy dip takes its inspiration from that tradition. It is very quick and easy to prepare and makes a wonderful start to any summer meal.

Simply put 250g/9oz of cooked beetroot in a food processor or blender, add 125ml/4fl oz/½ cup of plain yoghurt, 1 teaspoon of ground coriander, a pinch of ground ginger and a pinch of salt and blend to make a smooth purée. Stir in some lemon juice to taste, then serve accompanied by breadsticks or wedges of pitta bread for dipping.

**NOTES**

# Beetroot and chocolate cake

**Adding beetroot to this dark chocolate cake gives it a really rich, moist texture and a luscious, but not at all sickly, sweetness. The cinnamon and orange zest lend a subtle yet intriguing complexity to the overall flavour.**

**MAKES 1 x 20CM/8IN CAKE**
100g/3½oz dark chocolate
175g/6oz butter, at room temperature
175g/6oz soft brown sugar
3 eggs
175g/6oz self-raising flour
1 tsp baking powder
1-2 tbsp cocoa powder
1 tsp ground cinnamon
grated rind of 1 orange
1 large beetroot, about 150g/5½oz, peeled and grated

**FOR THE ICING**
100g/3½oz dark chocolate, chopped
100ml/3½fl oz/scant ½ cup double cream

Preheat the oven to 180°C/350°F/Gas 4. Lightly grease a 20cm/8in loose-based cake tin, then line the base with baking parchment or greaseproof paper.

Break the chocolate into small pieces and place in a bowl. Set over a pan of simmering water, so that the base of the bowl does not touch the water, and stir gently until the chocolate melts. Set aside to cool.

Beat the butter and sugar together until light and fluffy, then beat in the eggs one at a time, followed by the cooled chocolate. Sift over the flour, baking powder, cocoa and cinnamon and fold in carefully. Fold in the orange rind and beetroot.

Tip the cake mixture into the prepared tin and smooth the surface to make it even. Bake in the oven for about 50 minutes, until risen and a skewer inserted into the centre comes out clean. Turn out on to a wire rack and leave to cool.

Meanwhile, make the icing. Put the chocolate in a heatproof bowl. Heat the cream until almost boiling, then pour over the chocolate and leave to stand for about 5 minutes. Stir until the chocolate has melted and the mixture is smooth and creamy. Leave to cool slightly, until thick and glossy, then swirl on top of the cake.

# summer berries

Summer is always associated with an abundance of sweet fragrant berries. Strawberries and their vibrant red skins, speckled with tiny yellow seeds, arrive first, swiftly followed by soft succulent raspberries, with their velvety skin and deep pinkish-red hue, and fat juicy blueberries with their misty bloom. And there are a host of other less common berries too, including loganberries, youngberries, tayberries and boysenberries.

Most summer berries can simply be rinsed and eaten as they are, drenched with thick cream and perhaps a sprinkling of sugar, according to taste. However, they are also wonderfully versatile and can be added to fruit salads, cakes, muffins, tarts and pies. They are also perfect for decorating or piling on top of desserts such as meringues. And if you tire of eating them fresh, they can be preserved in jams and jellies or bottled in alcohol and sugar syrups.

## Summer berry pavlova (opposite)

**SERVES 6**

4 egg whites
225g/8oz caster sugar
2 tsp cornflour
1 tsp white-wine vinegar
300ml/10½fl oz/1¼ cups double cream
1 tsp vanilla extract
2 tbsp icing sugar, plus extra for dusting
500g/1lb 2oz mixed summer berries, such as blueberries, strawberries and raspberries, hulled and rinsed

Preheat the oven to 140°C/275°F/Gas 1. Line a baking sheet with greaseproof paper and mark out a 25cm/10in-diameter circle on it.

Whisk the egg whites in a clean bowl until they form stiff peaks. Gradually fold in the caster sugar, a tablespoon at a time, folding in the cornflour and vinegar with the last portion of sugar.

Spoon the meringue on to the baking sheet, inside the marked circle, flatten a little and make an indentation in the centre. Bake for about 1¼ hours in the oven until firm.

Remove from the oven, leave to cool, then carefully peel off the paper and place the meringue on a flat plate.

Whip the cream until it stands in soft peaks, then stir in the vanilla extract. Sift over and fold in the icing sugar. Spoon on to the meringue and pile the berries on top. Dust lightly with icing sugar and serve.

**NOTES**

# Raspberry millefeuille

**SERVES 4**

flour, for dusting
250g/9oz puff pastry
325ml/11fl oz/1⅓ cups crème fraîche
3 tbsp lemon curd
300g/10½oz raspberries, rinsed
icing sugar, for dusting

Preheat the oven to 200°C/400°F/Gas 6. Lightly grease two baking sheets. On a lightly floured surface, roll out the pastry to about 5mm/¼in thick, then trim to a 30 x 15cm/12 x 6in rectangle. Slice the pastry into six rectangles of 10 x 7.5cm/4 x 3in and arrange these on the baking sheets. Bake in the oven for 10 minutes until puffed up and golden. Transfer to a wire rack to cool.

Meanwhile, fold the crème fraîche and lemon curd together, then leave in the fridge to chill until ready to assemble the pastries.

With a serrated knife, halve each pastry rectangle horizontally and arrange four on a serving platter. Spread each with a couple of spoonfuls of the lemon cream, then top with some raspberries and a second pastry rectangle. Repeat with more lemon cream and berries, then a third pastry rectangle. Dust with icing sugar and serve.

Summer

# Blueberry and almond muffins

**MAKES 12**

400g/14oz self-raising flour
150g/5½ oz caster sugar
2 eggs, beaten
125ml/4fl oz/½ cup milk
4 tbsp vegetable oil
¼ tsp almond essence (optional)
175g/6oz blueberries
2 tbsp flaked almonds

Preheat the oven to 200°C/400°F/Gas 6. Line a 12-hole muffin tin with paper cases.

Sift the flour and sugar together into a large mixing bowl. Make a well in the centre and set aside.

Put the eggs, milk, oil and almond essence, if using, in a jug and beat together to combine. Pour into the well in the flour mixture and stir vigorously to combine. It does not matter if the mixture is a little lumpy.

Drop a tablespoon of the mixture into the bottom of each paper case, then sprinkle on a few blueberries. Top with the remaining mixture, then more blueberries, pressing them gently into the batter. Sprinkle a few almond flakes over each muffin.

Bake in the oven for about 20 minutes until risen and golden. Transfer to a wire rack to cool slightly before serving.

**NOTES**

# Baby summer puddings

**SERVES 4**

6 thin slices day-old white bread,
crusts removed
500g/1lb 2oz mixed summer
berries, such as raspberries,
strawberries, blueberries,
blackcurrants and redcurrants
about 4 tsp caster sugar
3 tbsp water
juice of ¼ lemon
thick cream, to serve

Trim the bread slices and use to line the base and sides of four small dariole moulds or ramekins (about 185ml/6fl oz each). Cut out four rounds from the remaining bread to fit inside the top of the moulds and set aside.

Prepare the fruit by removing any stems, leaves and hulls and cutting any large berries into halves or quarters. Put in a pan and sprinkle over the sugar and water. Cover tightly and heat very gently, shaking occasionally, for 5 minutes, until the berries start to release their juices. Increase the heat slightly and cook for a further 4 minutes, shaking the pan frequently, until the juices are released and syrupy.

Remove from the heat, check the flavouring and add the lemon juice and more sugar if necessary. Leave to cool slightly, then spoon the fruit with a little juice into the bread-lined moulds. Reserve any remaining juice.

Place one of the reserved rounds of bread on top of each pudding, then put a small saucer on top of that and weigh it down with something heavy. Chill in the fridge for at least 4 hours.

To serve, run a knife between each pudding and its mould and carefully turn out on to serving plates. Spoon any reserved juice over the top and serve with thick cream.

## marinated strawberries

Marinating strawberries with a drizzle of sweet, caramely balsamic vinegar really helps to bring out their sweetness and produces a wonderfully rich flavour.

To prepare, hull and halve 500g/1lb 2oz of ripe strawberries, then sprinkle over 1 teaspoon of caster sugar and 1½ teaspoons of balsamic vinegar. Toss to combine, then cover the bowl and chill for about 1 hour before serving. Try them with ice cream or a slice of vanilla cheesecake or a creamy panna cotta, or just as they are.

# currants

Tiny, jewel-like currants – glossy black, ruby red and creamy white – are among the delights of late summer. They look stunning piled on top of fresh fruit tarts, cakes, pavlovas and other desserts and add a delicious, sharp tang when mixed with sweeter, softer berries, such as strawberries. Although each type has a distinct individual flavour, all currants are tart. Whitecurrants, being the least acidic, are pleasant eaten raw, but in general currants are best served cooked – in sauces, in desserts (such as summer pudding, see page 115) and in jams and jellies. Currant sauces and jellies are frequently served with game, the tartness of the fruit making a good foil for the richness of the meat.

Buy only plump, shiny currants. To prepare, simply strip the berries from their stalks. The easiest way to do this is to hold the stalk by the stem, then strip it through the tines of a fork, so that the currants are gently pulled off.

## Blackcurrant sorbet

**SERVES 4-6**
450g/1lb blackcurrants, rinsed and trimmed, plus extra to decorate
300ml/10½fl oz/1¼ cups water
150g/5½oz caster sugar
3 tbsp crème de cassis liqueur
1 egg white

Put the blackcurrants in a pan with half the water. Cover and simmer for about 5 minutes, until the fruit is tender. Set aside to cool slightly.

Put the cooled currants in a food processor or blender and process to make a smooth purée, then press through a sieve to remove any debris. Chill in the fridge for at least 1 hour.

Meanwhile, put the remaining water and the sugar in a pan and heat, stirring, until the sugar has dissolved. Remove from the heat and leave to cool, then chill. When the purée and syrup are thoroughly chilled, stir together with the crème de cassis.

Pour the mixture into an ice-cream maker and churn until thick, then add the egg white and continue churning until the mixture is thick enough to scoop.

To make by hand, freeze the mixture for 4 hours then blend in a food processor until smooth. Lightly whisk the egg white until frothy, fold into the mixture, then freeze until firm.

Serve decorated with fresh blackcurrants.

**NOTES**

# gooseberries

Although it is the tart green fruits that most people think of when gooseberries are mentioned, there are golden and red varieties too – all of them perfect for summer desserts. The early-season green gooseberries are tart and sharp and should be cooked until tender with plenty of sugar. However, the ripe golden and red gooseberries can be sweet and mild and may be eaten raw. Cooked gooseberries are commonly paired with fragrant elderflowers – their white clustered heads can be seen growing in hedgerows alongside country fields and lanes.

Gooseberries are frequently used in pies, tarts and creamy fools, and preserved in jams and jellies. They can also be made into a wonderfully tart sauce, which is a popular accompaniment to grilled mackerel, contrasting well with the oiliness of the fish.

To prepare gooseberries, simply top and tail them with a pair of kitchen scissors, then use them according to the recipe. If you are making a purée by sieving the cooked berries, you can miss out the topping and tailing as the debris will be removed with straining.

## Gooseberry fool

**You will need different quantities of sugar according to the type of gooseberry you use – and personal taste, of course – so just keep adding sugar once the berries are cooked to attain the desired sweet-sour balance.**

**SERVES 4**
450g/1lb gooseberries, topped and tailed
2 tbsp water
sugar, to taste
125ml/4fl oz/½ cup double cream
150ml/5fl oz/⅔ cup Greek yoghurt

Put the gooseberries and water in a pan, cover and heat over a low heat until the juices start to run. Uncover, bring to the boil, then reduce the heat and simmer for about 10 minutes, stirring occasionally, until tender.

Remove from the heat, mash and stir in sugar to taste, then leave to cool completely.

Whip the cream in a large bowl, then fold the Greek yoghurt into it, followed by the cooled gooseberries. Serve cold or chilled.

**NOTES**

# Gooseberry and elderflower preserve

**Tart gooseberries and fragrant elderflowers are a classic pairing. Serve this delicious preserve for an elegant traditional afternoon tea, spread generously on thick slices of bread and butter or glistening of top of homemade scones with clotted cream.**

**MAKES ABOUT 2KG/4½LB**

1kg/2¼lb gooseberries, topped and tailed
250ml/9fl oz/1 cup water
1kg/2¼lb granulated sugar
juice of 1 lemon
flowers from 4 elderflower heads

Put the gooseberries in a large pan and pour over the water. Bring to the boil, reduce the heat, cover and leave to simmer for about 20 minutes, until the fruit is tender, then crush it using the back of a spoon.

Add the sugar, lemon juice and elderflowers and stir over a low heat until the sugar has dissolved. Boil for about 10 minutes until the temperature reaches 105°C/220°F on a sugar thermometer, then skim off any scum from the surface. Leave to cool for 5–10 minutes, then ladle into sterilized jars and seal.

## elderflowers

The white clustered flowers of the elderberry tree have an intense, perfumed flavour. They can be used in many recipes to add a delicious scented touch. A few flowerheads may be added to the pan when making jam, for instance, and stirred in until enough flavour has been imparted. Then fish out the flowers and continue making the jam in the usual way. They are also commonly used to prepare a cordial, that is diluted with sparking mineral water to make a refreshing drink, or used to flavour desserts. Use only flowers with creamy open petals that are not yet beginning to drop.

To prepare elderflower cordial, put 900g/2lb of sugar in a large bowl and pour over 2.5 litres/4 pints/10 cups of boiling water. Stir to dissolve, then leave to cool. Stir in 1 packet of citric acid (available from chemists), then rinse 30 elderflower heads and add to the sugar syrup with 2 thinly sliced lemons. Leave to stand for 24 hours, stirring occasionally. Strain the liquid through muslin and bottle. This cordial freezes well too.

# cherries

The arrival of cherry blossom always seems to mark the beginning of spring and, in the same way, the arrival of shiny plump cherries, piled high on the greengrocers' shelves, tells us that summer is truly here. From creamy yellow through bright red to dark purple-black, these wonderful fruits, hanging in twos and threes from long narrow stalks, are the ultimate seasonal treat. They may be sweet or sour according to variety – although only the sweet ones are usually on sale – and the flesh can vary from firm and crisp to soft and juicy.

Sweet cherries are usually eaten raw, while the intensely flavoured sour ones are reserved for cooking – mainly in preserves – or for making liqueurs. Cherries have a natural affinity with chocolate and the two ingredients feature together in numerous desserts, most famously in the creamy chocolate cake Black Forest gâteau. Fresh cherries may be stoned and folded into cake batter before baking. The stoned fruits are also good in pies, tarts, strudels and other baked desserts, or frozen into sorbets and ice creams. They make a sharp fruity sauce to serve with game and, in Eastern Europe, are widely used to make sweet-and-sour soups and as a stuffing for dumplings.

Buy only plump glossy fruits with unblemished skins and flexible green stalks. Any with browning or brittle stalks indicate that the cherries were picked quite some time before. Flavour can vary enormously, so, if you can, taste before you buy. Cherries take little preparation and should simply be washed and plucked from their stalk. Some recipes require the stones to be removed. The easiest way to do this is with a cherry stoner, in which the cherry sits in a tiny cup and a bar is pressed through the centre of the fruit, pushing out the stone. If you do not have a cherry stoner, cut around the stone (as you would for larger stoned fruits, such as peaches and apricots), then gently pull away the flesh and prise out the stone.

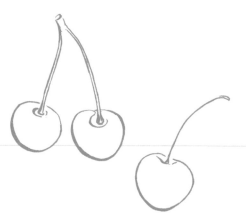

**NOTES**

# Cherry chocolate brownies

**Dark chocolate and juicy cherries are natural partners and these luscious brownies - sweet, sticky and studded with fresh cherries - are truly indulgent. Serve them unadorned, or with thick cream or ice cream. When fresh cherries are out of season, use drained preserved cherries (see page 123), substituting the kirsch with the preserving liqueur.**

**MAKES 16**
200g/7oz dark chocolate
200g/7oz butter
3 eggs
200g/7oz caster sugar
2 tbsp kirsch liqueur
70g/2½oz self-raising flour
200g/7oz fresh cherries, stoned

Preheat the oven to 180°C/350°F/Gas 4. Grease a 22.5cm/9in square baking tin and line with greaseproof paper.

Put the chocolate and butter in a heatproof bowl. Place over a pan of simmering water, so that the base of the bowl does not touch the water, and warm, stirring, until the chocolate has nearly melted. Remove from the heat and continue stirring until the chocolate has completely melted. Set aside to cool for about 5 10 minutes.

Beat the eggs into the chocolate mixture, one at a time, then stir in the sugar and kirsch. Sift over the flour, then fold it in. Fold in the cherries. Turn the mixture into the lined tin and spread out evenly. Bake in the oven for about 30 minutes, until pale and slightly crackled on top and just firm to the touch.

Leave the brownies to cool in the tin, then cut into squares.

## chocolate-dipped cherries

Fresh cherries dipped in either dark or white chocolate make wonderful *petits fours* to serve with coffee after a special dinner. They are also quick and easy to prepare. Simply break some chocolate into small pieces and place in a heatproof bowl. Set the bowl over a pan of simmering water, making sure the base does not touch the water, and stir gently until the chocolate has melted. Remove the bowl from the heat. Holding each cherry by its stem, dip the bottom half into the melted chocolate, then place on a baking sheet lined with greaseproof paper. Leave in a cool place to set, then chill in the fridge until ready to serve.

# Clafoutis _(opposite)_

**This melt-in-the-mouth, custardy French batter pudding is a wonderful way to make the most of the glut of fresh cherries available during their brief season. Traditionally it is made with a particular variety of black cherry known as a _guine_, but any type of black cherry can be used here to make a heavenly dessert. Some prefer to stone the cherries before adding them to the dish for ease of eating, but leaving them in gives a better flavour.**

**SERVES 4-6**

butter, for greasing
300g/10½oz black cherries
40g/1½oz plain flour
50g/1¾oz caster sugar
6 large eggs, beaten
200ml/7fl oz/generous ¾ cup milk
200ml/7fl oz/generous ¾ cup single cream
2 tbsp kirsch liqueur
icing sugar, for dusting

Preheat the oven to 190°C/375°F/Gas 5. Butter a round baking dish, about 20cm/8in in diameter, and scatter the cherries in the bottom.

Combine the flour and sugar in a bowl, then gradually beat in the eggs until smooth. Whisk in the milk and cream, then stir in the kirsch. Pour this batter over the cherries and bake in the oven for about 50 minutes until golden and puffed up. It should still have a wobble, but a knife inserted in the centre should come out clean. Serve hot or warm, dusted with icing sugar.

## preserving cherries

Cherries are in season for only a few short months, so it is well worth preserving them in jams, jellies and other sweet and savoury preserves when they are available in abundance. They may be bottled in sugar and alcohol to make a sweet cherry liqueur, the alcohol-spiked cherries being a glorious addition to chocolate cakes, ice cream and other creamy desserts. They even make lovely sour pickles, when preserved with vinegar and spices, to serve with red meats and game.

To preserve cherries in brandy, wash and stone about 450g/1lb of cherries and pack into a wide-necked bottle or jar, sprinkling over 6 tablespoons of granulated sugar as you go. Pour over enough brandy to cover and seal tightly. Store in a cool, dark place for at least 1 month, shaking the bottle occasionally, before serving.

# apricots

Native to China, peachy orange apricots with their velvety skin thrive in warmer climates. Arriving for a brief season in early summer, they are generally best cooked - either poached, baked or roasted - so that the flesh becomes meltingly tender and juicy with a sweet yet refreshingly sharp flavour.

Try them in compotes and fruit salads, tarts and pies and cakes and crumbles, or make them into ice creams and mousses. They are delicious preserved in jellies and jams - stirring just a spoonful or two of homemade apricot jam through plain yoghurt makes a quick and simple dessert that can be enjoyed at any time of the year.

Large quantities of apricots are also preserved by drying, which often helps to intensify their flavour. Dried apricots are a popular additon to many savoury dishes, such as meat stews and pilafs, and are mixed into stuffings for meat and poultry, as in many Middle Eastern recipes.

Select firm ripe fruits with an almost glowing colour and avoid any that are bruised, blemished or have a greenish tinge. To remove the stone, cut around the crease of the fruit using a sharp knife, then twist the two halves apart and prise out the stone.

## roast apricots

One of the simplest and most delicious ways to enjoy apricots is to roast them. They can then be served hot from the oven with a big dollop of crème fraîche, or served cold, stirred into plain yoghurt or with ice cream. They are also delicious on slices of toasted *panettone* or raisin bread for breakfast.

To prepare, allow 3 apricots per person. Halve and stone them, then arrange, cut-side up, in a baking dish. Sprinkle a few teaspoons of caster sugar over each half of fruit and then bake in a preheated oven at 200°C/400°F/Gas 6 for about 30 minutes until tender and juicy.

NOTES

# Apricot and almond tart

**Juicy tart apricots and sweet crunchy almonds are a classic combination – as you will soon realize for good reason, when you tuck into this sublime tart.**

**SERVES 6-8**

115g/4oz butter, at room temperature
115g/4oz caster sugar
2 eggs
115g/4oz ground almonds
grated rind of ½ lemon
300g/10½oz fresh apricots, halved and stoned
icing sugar, for dusting

**FOR THE PASTRY**

115g/4oz plain flour, plus extra for dusting
½ tbsp caster sugar
55g/2oz butter, chilled and diced
about 1 tbsp cold water

First make the pastry. Put the flour and sugar in a food processor and pulse to combine. Add the butter and pulse until the mixture resembles fine breadcrumbs. With the motor running, gradually add just enough water until the mixture comes together. Press into a ball, wrap in clear film and leave in the fridge to chill for at least 30 minutes.

Preheat the oven to 190°C/375°F/Gas 5. On a lightly floured surface, roll out the pastry and use to line a 20cm/8in tart tin. Cover with foil and baking beans and bake in the oven for 10 minutes. Remove the foil and beans and bake for a further 5-10 minutes until the base is dry. Remove from the oven and lower the temperature to 180°C/350°F/Gas 4.

Meanwhile, beat the butter and sugar together in a large bowl, then beat in the eggs, one at a time. Fold in the ground almonds and lemon rind, then spoon the mixture into the prepared pastry case. Arrange the apricots in the tart, gently pressing them into the almond mixture. Bake for about 35 minutes, until firm and golden brown. Serve warm or cold, lightly dusted with icing sugar.

## apricot and marzipan filo parcels

To make a simple and delicious dessert for four people, cut 8 apricots in half and remove the stones. Place a piece of marzipan into the gap left by the stone in each fruit, then press the apricot halves back together around it. Take 2 sheets of filo pastry, brush with melted butter then place one on top of the other and trim into a 20cm/8in square. Put an apricot in the centre, pull up the pastry around the fruit and twist to form a small parcel. Repeat with more pastry sheets and the rest of the apricots. Brush with more butter, then arrange on a baking sheet and bake in a preheated oven at 180°C/350°F/Gas 4 for about 25 minutes until crisp and golden. Serve warm, lightly dusted with icing sugar.

# peaches and nectarines

Succulent peaches and nectarines require plenty of sunshine to develop their luscious sweetness and are at their best when left to ripen fully on the tree. The two fruits are similar in taste and texture and can generally be substituted for each other. The main difference is in their skin. Peaches are covered in a soft downy bloom while the skin of nectarines is smooth and glossy like that of plums. Both fruits may have either white or yellow flesh, the white-fleshed varieties generally being considered to have the better flavour.

Delicious eaten straight from the tree, they can also be sliced or chopped and added to salads and desserts. They are good cooked, too - poached, grilled or roasted and baked into pies, crumbles and cobblers, or preserved by simply bottling in syrup or alcohol or making into jam.

Choose unblemished fruits that give slightly when squeezed gently in the palm of the hand. If peeled peaches or nectarines are required, place the fruits in a heatproof bowl and pour over boiling water. Leave to stand for about 15 seconds. Drain, then slip off and discard the skins.

## Peaches in white wine and vanilla syrup

**SERVES 4**
4 peaches, about 675g/1½lb in total
350ml/12fl oz/1½ cups white wine
225g/8oz granulated sugar
1 vanilla pod
3 tbsp brandy
thick cream or ice cream, to serve

Put the peaches in a large heatproof bowl and pour over boiling water to cover. Leave for about 15 seconds, then drain and peel away the skins. Halve, and remove and discard the stones.

Put the wine and sugar in a pan. Split the vanilla pod lengthways, then add to the pan. Heat, stirring, until the sugar has dissolved. Bring to the boil and allow to bubble for 5 minutes, then add the prepared peaches, cover and simmer for 5-10 minutes until the fruit is just tender.

Remove the peaches from the pan and place in a serving bowl, then remove and discard the vanilla pod. Boil the syrup for 5-10 minutes until reduced and slightly thickened. Remove from the heat, stir in the brandy and pour over the peaches. Leave to cool. Serve at room temperature or chilled with cream or ice cream.

**NOTES**

# melons

Available from summer to early autumn, fragrant melons, with their refreshing honeyed flesh, grow on trailing vines and come in many guises: cantaloupes, with their ridged rind and apricot-tinted flesh; charentais, with their delicate orange-coloured interior; galias, with their pale green flesh and crumpled skin; honeydews, bright yellow and elongated like a rugby ball; and watermelons, with their thirst-quenching, bright-red flesh – to name but a few. Melons vary enormously in size too. Some are just big enough for one or two people, while others, such as watermelons, can be huge and are often sold cut into wedges rather than whole. Usually eaten raw, they can be perfect on their own, or simply sprinkled with a little ground ginger, or spiked with a few drops of alcohol. The flesh is also good sliced or chopped into salads, or juiced with other fruits and vegetables. It is delicious puréed and blended into chilled summer soups, turned into sorbets or used to make melon jam. The rind, which is usually discarded, can even be preserved in vinegar and spices and served as a pickle.

Choose fruits that feel heavy for their size. When ripe, most melons have a strong fragrant aroma, so try to hold and smell them before buying. Avoid those with little or no scent or a musky smell which indicates that the fruit may be over-ripe. To prepare, halve small melons and cut larger ones into wedges. Then scoop out and discard the seeds. In watermelons, the seeds are embedded in the flesh and can be easily removed with a pointed knife.

### spiked watermelon

Alcohol-spiked melon is great for a summer party. Use an apple corer or long vegetable peeler to make six bore-holes in the top of a melon, reserving the cored-out pieces. Press a wooden skewer into each bore-hole several times at different angles to make fine channels into the flesh. Pour vodka into each bore-hole and leave the melon to absorb the spirit. Top up from time to time, using about 500ml/17fl oz/2 cups vodka in total. Replace the removed pieces and leave in a cool place overnight. Serve sliced into wedges.

summer

**NOTES**

# Cantaloupe and feta salad

**This light refreshing salad of sweet juicy melon, studded with cubes of salty cheese, makes a delicious summer appetizer. You can use any kind of melon but fragrant cantaloupe, with its apricot-coloured flesh, looks particularly attractive.**

**SERVES 4**

juice and grated rind of ½ lemon
pinch of sugar
3 tbsp olive oil
freshly ground black pepper
2 tsp finely chopped fresh mint leaves
2 ripe cantaloupe melons
115g/4oz feta cheese, cut into bite-size cubes
2 tbsp pinenuts, toasted

Make a dressing by whisking together the lemon juice and rind, sugar and olive oil in a small bowl. Season to taste with pepper, stir in the chopped mint and set aside.

Cut the cantaloupes in half and scoop out the seeds. Then cut into wedges and slice off and discard the skin. Chop the wedges of melon flesh into bite-size chunks.

Divide the melon among four serving plates and scatter over the feta cheese and pinenuts. Drizzle over the dressing and serve.

# Melon sorbet

**Use a ripe scented melon with a good flavour for this sorbet. Any kind will do - galias, cantaloupes and watermelons all work equally well.**

**SERVES 4**

2 tbsp caster sugar
4 tbsp water
1 melon, about 675g/1½lb
juice of 1 lime
few sprigs of fresh mint, to decorate

Put the sugar and water in a pan and heat gently, stirring, until the sugar dissolves, then bring to the boil. Remove from the heat and set aside to cool.

Cut the melon into wedges, scoop out the seeds, then cut the melon flesh from the skin. Chop the flesh into rough chunks, then place in a food processor or blender and process to make a smooth purée. Stir in the cooled sugar syrup and lime juice.

Churn the mixture in an ice-cream maker until it is thick and smooth, then freeze until firm and scoopable. Serve, decorated with sprigs of fresh mint.

# Autumn

After long days of summer sunshine, the coolness of autumn ushers in a bumper harvest. Golden-orange squashes, sweet potatoes, earthy wild mushrooms, aniseedy fennel and crisp celery all come into season. They are perfect for cooking up into more substantial dishes as the temperatures begins to drop. Wild game is also one of the many pleasures that arrive with autumn. Venison, rabbit, duck, quail, pheasant and pigeon are just a few of the treats on offer - each with its own robust and distinctive flavour and perfect for roasting, braising or stewing with the many and varied seasonal vegetables and fruits. The appearance of plump honeyed figs, purple-bloomed plums and scented grapes may mark the end of summer's glut of berries, but they are a wonderful way to welcome in the new season. Jewel-like pomegranates are a joy to the eye, as well as adding a refreshing tang to both sweet and savoury dishes. There are heaps of apples and pears, and the hedgerows are bulging with wild fruits, just waiting to be picked and turned into jams and jellies.

# onions

Onions are available from cold-storage at any time of the year, but appear in the shops freshly harvested only from late summer until late autumn. They are one of those true kitchen essentials. Virtually every savoury recipe – from soups, sauces and stews to curries and tagines – uses onions as a flavouring. But they are more than just a necessary addition to a dish; they can also be the central feature, as the many superb recipes for onion soups, onion tarts, roasted and stuffed onions, onion bhajis and crispy fried onion rings all demonstrate. As a general rule, most onions have a crisp, juicy texture and powerful, pungent flavour when raw, but become soft, mild and sweet when cooked.

There are many different varieties of onion, all with their own distinctive characteristics. Brown onions with their thickish skins are the real kitchen standby. Their strong flavour mellows to an almost caramel-like sweetness when they are gently fried. Large, round Spanish – or yellow – onions have a much milder flavour that becomes honeyed with long slow cooking. Red onions are milder still, making them ideal for using raw or in dishes that require only a short cooking time. White onions, with their papery skin and white flesh, usually have a fairly pungent flavour. Smaller onions, such as the tiny white pearl variety and the distinctive flat cipolla – or *borettane* – onions are usually used whole for pickling or in stews.

When buying, select only firm onions, avoiding any that are damaged or starting to soften. They keep well, so it is worth buying a string of them. Hang this somewhere suitably cool and dark, and it should last for several months.

Onions are nearly always peeled before using. They can be cooked whole, sliced or chopped. To peel large onions, simply slice off the top and bottom, then make a shallow slit in the skin and peel it away. To peel smaller onions, slice off the top and bottom as for larger onions, then soak in boiling water for about 3 minutes to loosen the skins, which should then slip off easily.

**NOTES**

# Pissaladière

**This classic French tart, topped with meltingly sweet onions and salty anchovies and olives, is often made with a pastry base, but it is equally good on a crisp yeasted dough.**

**SERVES 6**
2 tbsp olive oil
3 Spanish onions, thinly sliced
2 cloves garlic, sliced
4-6 fresh sage leaves, chopped
salt and freshly ground black pepper
50g/1¾oz can anchovies, drained and halved lengthways
large handful of juicy black olives
handful of sultanas

**FOR THE YEAST DOUGH**
300g/10½oz strong white bread flour, plus extra for dusting
½ tsp salt
1½ tsp easy-blend dried yeast
185ml/6fl oz/¾ cup warm water
2 tbsp olive oil

First make the yeast dough. Combine the flour, salt and yeast in a bowl and make a well in the centre. Pour the water and oil into the well and gradually mix in the flour mixture to make a soft, but not sticky, dough. Tip out on to a lightly floured surface and knead for about 10 minutes, until smooth and elastic. Place in a clean bowl, cover with clear film and leave to rise for about 45 minutes, until doubled in size.

Meanwhile, heat the oil in a pan, add the onions and garlic and cook gently over a very low heat for about 25 minutes, stirring frequently, until very tender and collapsed. Sprinkle over the sage, season with salt and pepper and remove from the heat.

Preheat the oven to 220°C/425°F/Gas 7 and grease a baking sheet. Roll out the dough to form a rectangle about 30 x 25cm/ 12 x 10in. Place on the baking sheet, spread with the onion mixture, then arrange the anchovies and olives on top. Bake in the oven for about 10 minutes, then scatter over the sultanas and return to the oven for a further 10 minutes, until the dough is golden and crispy. Serve warm, cut into slices.

## french onion soup

This satisfying soup is a perfect way to welcome in the first onions of autumn. Topped with cheesy croûtes, it is almost a meal in itself. The secret to the rich colour and flavour lies in caramelizing the onions. To prepare, cook about 6 thinly sliced onions in 2 tablespoons of olive oil over a low heat, stirring frequently, for about 20 minutes, until the onions are very soft. Stir in a sprinkling of fresh thyme, a good pinch of soft brown sugar and 2 tablespoons of balsamic vinegar, then continue cooking and stirring for another 20 minutes, until the mixture is dark and sticky – don't let it burn. Stir in 1 tablespoon of flour, then gradually add 1 litre/1¾ pints/4 cups of beef or vegetable stock and a large glass of white wine. Simmer, covered, for 15 minutes, then check and adjust the seasoning.

Make the croûtes by heating 115g/4oz of Gruyère cheese, a splash of white wine and a little Dijon mustard together in a pan until the cheese melts. Off the heat, beat in an egg yolk. Spoon this mixture over 4 thick slices of toasted baguette that have been rubbed with garlic and grill these until golden and bubbling. Serve the soup piping hot, with a cheesy croûte floating on top of each bowl.

# Creamy red onion and Parmesan tart (opposite)

**Onions make the perfect filling for savoury tarts and pies - and red ones are wonderful, as here, roasted until sweet and caramelized and paired with a garlicky, cheesy egg custard.**

**SERVES 6**

4 tbsp milk
80ml/2½ fl oz/⅓ cup single cream
2 cloves garlic, halved
2 red onions
2 tbsp olive oil
1 tbsp balsamic vinegar
salt and freshly ground black pepper
1 egg yolk
1 tbsp plain flour, plus extra for dusting
25g/1oz Parmesan cheese, grated
375g/13oz puff pastry
handful of black olives
2 tsp capers, rinsed and patted dry
leaves from 2-3 sprigs of fresh thyme

Preheat the oven to 200°C/400°F/Gas 6. Grease a baking sheet. Put the milk, cream and garlic in a pan and bring to the boil, then remove from the heat and leave to stand for 15 minutes.

Meanwhile, peel the red onions, keeping the root intact, cut each one into 6-8 wedges and arrange in a roasting tin. Whisk together the oil and vinegar, drizzle over the onions and turn them to coat. Season with salt and pepper and roast in the oven for 15 minutes. Remove from the oven, set aside and reduce the temperature to 190°C/375°F/Gas 5.

Whisk together the egg yolk and flour in a heatproof bowl to make a smooth paste. Bring the milk and cream back to simmering point, then remove the garlic and discard. Gradually pour the hot milk and cream into the egg and flour mixture, whisking continuously, until well combined and really smooth. Return to the pan and heat gently for about 3 minutes, stirring constantly, until thick and creamy. Remove from the heat, stir in the Parmesan cheese and season to taste with salt and pepper.

Roll out the pastry on a lightly floured surface, cut out a 25cm/10in round and place on the baking sheet. Spread the cheesy custard over the pastry, leaving a 2cm/¾in border all the way round, then arrange the roasted onions on top. Scatter over the olives and capers and bake in the oven for about 25 minutes, until the pastry is crisp and golden. Serve, sprinkled with the thyme leaves.

**NOTES**

# celery

Coming into season in autumn, the long, ribbed stems of the celery plant are refreshingly crisp and may be white or green. The green version has been grown in full light, while the paler form has been cultivated covered by a light coating of earth to achieve a more delicate flavour.

Delicious cooked or raw, celery is an essential ingredient in most stocks and is good added to stews. On cooking, the crunchy texture becomes soft and silky and the flavour mellows. Left raw, it can be sliced and added to salads, such as the famous apple and walnut Waldorf salad, or eaten simply as sticks. Celery sticks make the perfect tool for scooping up dips and are a great partner to those made with with cheese, particularly blue cheese (see below).

When buying, always look for firm, crisp heads and avoid any with blemishes, brown spots or mushy patches. Celery should be used as soon as possible after buying, although it may be placed, root-end down, in a jug of cold water and stored in a cool place for several days.

To prepare celery, cut off the root, separate the head into sticks and wash well to remove all traces of earth or grit. Celery is often 'stringy', so strip out and pull off any strings as you trim off the root end. White celery tends to be stringier than green.

## celery and blue-cheese dip

By partnering this creamy, piquant blue-cheese dip with crisp sticks of fresh celery – and perhaps a few handfuls of grapes – you will have a delicious appetizer that takes only minutes to prepare.

To make, simply crumble 200g/7oz blue cheese into a bowl and add 125ml/4fl oz/½ cup crème fraîche. Season to taste with black pepper and beat thoroughly until really smooth and creamy. Chill in the fridge until ready to serve.

**NOTES**

# Celery soup

**SERVES 4**
25g/1oz butter
2 onions, finely chopped
2 tbsp flour
800ml/28fl oz/3¼ cups
vegetable stock
600g/1lb 5oz celery, trimmed
and sliced
400ml/14fl oz/1⅔ cups milk
60ml/2fl oz//¼ cup crème fraîche
salt and freshly ground black
pepper

Melt the butter in a pan and gently fry the onions for about 5 minutes. Stir in the flour and cook, stirring, for about 1 minute, then gradually stir in the stock.

Add the celery, bring to the boil, then reduce the heat, cover and simmer gently for about 15 minutes.

Using a slotted spoon, remove about 3 large spoonfuls of celery and set aside. Pour the rest of the soup into a food processor or blender and blend until smooth.

Return the soup to the pan, add the reserved celery and the milk and heat until just simmering. Remove from the heat, stir in the crème fraîche, season to taste and serve.

# Braised pheasant with celery

**Celery, with its faintly salty flavour, is a classic partner for gamey pheasant and is wonderful cooked in white wine and served with a creamy sauce.**

**SERVES 4**
25g/1oz butter
2 pheasants, cleaned
3 rashers of streaky bacon, snipped
into small pieces
250ml/9fl oz/1 cup chicken stock
250ml/9fl oz/1 cup white wine
450g/1lb celery, trimmed and sliced
1 tbsp cornflour, blended with
1 tbsp cold water
4 tbsp crème fraîche
large handful of fresh flat-leaf
parsley, roughly chopped
salt and freshly ground black pepper

Preheat the oven to 180°C/350°F/Gas 4. Melt the butter in a large pan. Add the pheasants and brown all over, then transfer to a heatproof casserole dish, breast-side down. Scatter over the bacon pieces, pour over the stock and wine, cover and cook in the oven for about 30 minutes. Turn over the pheasants and add the celery, tucking it in around the birds. Cover and cook for a further 30 minutes, until the birds are cooked through.

Transfer the pheasants and celery to a serving dish and keep warm. Place the casserole over a low heat, add the cornflour mixture to the cooking liquid and cook, stirring, until thickened. Stir in the crème fraîche and parsley, season to taste with salt and pepper and transfer to a jug or gravy boat to serve alongside the pheasant and celery.

# fennel

Florence fennel, with its ridged greenish-white bulbs topped by a flourish of feathery fronds, was first cultivated in Italy in the 17th century. The crisp raw flesh is refreshingly juicy with a hint of aniseed. Fennel softens with cooking but still retains its distinctive flavour. Although good raw in salads - particularly when paired with juicy orange segments - it is also popular braised, steamed, roasted or grilled and served as a vegetable. Add it to soups, coat in a creamy sauce, or smother with crème fraîche, sprinkle with Parmesan cheese and bake to make a mouthwatering gratin.

Buy small bulbs with a fresh white colour, vibrant green leaves and no blemishes or soft brown patches. It is usually necessary to remove the outer layer of flesh. Then slice the rest - either thinly for tossing into salads, or cut into thicker slices, halves or quarters, ready for cooking.

Thin slices or chunks, brushed with olive oil and sprinkled with lemon juice and seasoning, make a wonderful addition to any summer barbecue.

## Poussin baked with fennel and vermouth

**SERVES 4**
juice of 1 lemon
2 cloves garlic, crushed
3 tbsp olive oil
salt and freshly ground black pepper
2 poussins
3 heads of fennel
80ml/2½fl oz/⅓ cup vermouth

Preheat the oven to 190°C/375°F/Gas 5. Whisk together the lemon juice, garlic and olive oil in small bowl, season to taste with salt and pepper and set aside.

Season the poussins with salt and pepper and put in a roasting tin. Remove the green feathery fronds from the fennel and set aside. Slice the bulbs into quarters and arrange around the birds.

Pour the lemon and garlic mixture over the poussins and fennel and turn to coat all over. Grind over a little pepper, then pour the vermouth over the fennel. Bake in the oven for about 45 minutes, spooning the juices over the birds and fennel from time to time, until the poussins are cooked and the fennel tender. The poussins are cooked if the juices run clear when a sharp knife is inserted into the thickest part of the thigh. Serve, garnished with the reserved fennel fronds and the juices spooned over the top.

NOTES

# mushrooms

Wild mushrooms have a much stronger flavour than the cultivated varieties and come in a vast array of shapes and sizes. Ceps, also known as boletus or porcini, are probably the most prized of all wild mushrooms. They have fleshy pale-brown stalks and caps and an intensely nutty taste. They can be dried by slicing, laying on a tray in a single layer and placing in a warm place for several days. Once they have dried, store them in an airtight container; soak in hot water for about 30 minutes before using. Trumpet-shaped chanterelles are another highly valued mushroom, with an orangy hue and a distinctive, almost fruity, taste. They can also be dried and stored for later use. Blewits, with their bluish caps and lilac gills, are strikingly pretty and have a strong flavour that pairs well with similarly pungent ingredients such as onions and garlic. The large flat field mushroom, a close relative of the cultivated mushroom, is almost meaty in taste and texture.

As well as mushrooms, there are other edible wild fungi, the most lauded of all being the Piedmont or white truffle. Yellowish-brown with reddish mottled flesh and irregular in shape, these fungi grow underground and are so highly sought after that pigs and dogs are specially trained to hunt them out. They have a very distinctive, sweetly aromatic flavour and are usually finely sliced and cooked very quickly or shaved over a dish just before serving.

### simple mushroom pâté

This richly flavoured pâté makes a great appetizer or snack, served with crisp wafer-thin slices of toast. To make, melt a few knobs of butter in a pan, toss in 2 chopped cloves of garlic and cook gently for a minute or two. Stir in about 450g/1lb of roughly chopped mixed mushrooms, add a pinch of salt and cook for another 10 minutes, until the juices start to run. Tip into a blender or food processor and process briefly until finely chopped. Tranfer to a bowl, stir in 4 tablespoons of crème fraîche, a handful of fine breadcrumbs and a handful of chopped fresh flat-leaf parsley. Season to taste with freshly grated nutmeg, lemon juice, salt and freshly ground black pepper. Mix well and chill for at least an hour before serving.

NOTES

# Wild mushroom soup

**This rich, creamy soup, infused with aromatic sage, is perfect for serving as the weather begins to cool and you suddenly start to develop cravings for warming hearty food. Serve it piping hot, accompanied by chunks of warm, crusty bread, spread thickly with butter.**

**SERVES 4**

55g/2oz butter
1 onion, chopped
1 clove garlic, chopped
500g/1lb 2oz mixed wild mushrooms, roughly chopped
1 tbsp plain flour
125ml/4fl oz/½ cup white wine
1 litre/1¾ pints/4 cups vegetable stock
4 tbsp crème fraîche
handful of fresh sage leaves, chopped
2 tsp chopped fresh flat-leaf parsley
salt and freshly ground black pepper

Melt the butter in a pan, add the onion and garlic and cook over a gentle heat for about 5 minutes, until soft. Add the mushrooms and cook for a further 10 minutes.

Sprinkle the flour over the mushrooms and stir for about 1 minute. Gradually stir in the wine and stock and bring to the boil. Reduce the heat and leave to simmer for about 15 minutes.

Allow to cool slightly, then tip the mushroom mixture into a food processor or blender and process until smooth.

Heat through in a clean pan. Stir in the crème fraîche and the chopped sage and parsley, season to taste with salt and pepper and serve immediately.

# Wild mushroom pasta with spicy sausage

**SERVES 4**

6 spicy pork sausages
2 tbsp olive oil
1 onion, finely chopped
2 cloves garlic, crushed
600g/1lb 5oz mixed wild mushrooms, thickly sliced
salt and freshly ground black pepper
4 ripe plum tomatoes, peeled (see page 90), seeded and chopped
2 tsp chopped fresh sage
300g/10½oz fusilli or conchiglie pasta
freshly grated Parmesan cheese, to serve (optional)

Preheat the grill until hot. Arrange the sausages under the grill and cook for about 5 minutes on each side, until well browned. Slice into 1cm/½in-thick chunks and set aside.

Heat the olive oil in large pan. Add the onion and garlic and cook gently for about 5 minutes, until soft. Add the mushrooms, sprinkle over a pinch of salt and cook for about 10 minutes. Add the tomatoes, sage and sausage chunks and simmer gently for a further 10 minutes, stirring now and again.

Meanwhile, cook the pasta in a pan of boiling salted water, according to the instructions on the packet. Drain well.

Check the sauce for seasoning, then add the pasta and toss to combine. Serve immediately, sprinkled with a little Parmesan cheese, if liked.

# Wild mushroom risotto *(opposite)*

**SERVES 4**

3 tbsp vegetable oil
2 cloves garlic, finely chopped
500g/1lb 2oz mixed wild
mushrooms, sliced
salt and freshly ground black pepper
about 1.2 litres/2¾ pints/4¾ cups
vegetable stock
1 onion, finely chopped
275g/9½oz risotto rice
185ml/6fl oz/¾ cup white wine
handful of fresh chives, chopped,
plus extra to garnish
55g/2oz Parmesan cheese, grated,
plus shavings to serve

Heat half the oil in a large pan. Add half of the garlic and fry gently for about 1 minute. Add the mushrooms, sprinkle over a pinch of salt and cook gently until the mushrooms start to release their juices. Increase the heat and cook, stirring occasionally, for about 5 minutes, until the juices have evaporated. Set aside. In a separate pan, bring the stock to a gentle simmer.

Heat the remaining oil in another large pan, then add the onion and remaining garlic and fry gently for about 5 minutes. Add the risotto rice and cook, stirring, for 2 minutes. Add the wine and simmer, stirring, until nearly all the liquid has been absorbed. Add a ladleful of the hot stock and simmer, stirring, until nearly all the liquid has been absorbed. Add another ladleful of stock and continue cooking in this way for about 20 minutes, until the rice is tender but still has some bite. Just before the end of the cooking time, stir in the mushrooms.

Remove the pan from the heat, stir in the chopped chives and grated Parmesan cheese and season to taste with black pepper. Serve sprinkled with Parmesan shavings and more chives.

# Pork cooked with marsala and wild mushrooms

**SERVES 4**

25g/1oz butter
4 pork loin chops, about
200g/7oz each
2 cloves garlic, finely chopped
250g/9oz mixed wild
mushrooms, sliced
salt and freshly ground black pepper
4 tbsp marsala or sherry
¼ tsp fresh thyme leaves
2 tbsp double cream

Melt the butter in a pan, add the pork chops and brown for about 2-3 minutes on each side. Remove from the pan and set aside.

Add the garlic to the pan and fry gently for about 30 seconds, then add the mushrooms, sprinkle over a pinch of salt and cook for about 10 minutes until the juices have been released and have been slightly reduced.

Return the pork chops to the pan, pour over the marsala or sherry, stir in the thyme and bubble gently for 5-6 minutes, until the meat is cooked through. Remove the chops to warm serving plates. Stir the cream into the mushroom mixture, season with more salt, if needed, and pepper and serve spooned over the chops.

**NOTES**

# autumn squashes

Arriving in autumn (but known as "winter" squashes), cold-weather squashes are set apart from their summer cousins by their thick skins, orange or yellow flesh and large, tough seeds. There are many different types. The pumpkin, with its dazzling orange skin, is widely available, as is the creamy, smooth-skinned butternut squash and the smaller acorn squash, with its fluted dark-green or bright-orange skin. Less common are the hubbard, the onion and the Asian kabocha squash.

With their sweet flavour and smooth texture, all squashes are delicious sautéed, roasted, baked or steamed in their own juices and can be added to stews, pies and soups, used to stuff pasta or tossed into salads. Their natural sweetness also makes them ideal for using in cakes and pies, pumpkin pie being the classic dessert served at a US Thanksgiving dinner.

Buy only unblemished squashes that feel heavy for their size. Avoid really large ones, as they often lack flavour. To prepare, halve or cut into segments, then scoop out the seeds, which may be roasted, cracked open and eaten as a snack. If sautéeing or adding to a soup or stew, cut off the skin; if baking or roasting, remove the skin before or after cooking.

## Thai-style butternut squash curry

**SERVES 4**

2 cloves garlic, peeled
2.5cm/1in piece fresh ginger, peeled and grated
2 green chillies, seeded and chopped
3 shallots, chopped
4 kaffir lime leaves, shredded
2 lemongrass stalks, chopped
2 tbsp sunflower oil
600ml/1 pint/2½ cups vegetable stock
150g/5½oz cashew nuts
1 tsp Thai fish sauce
½ tsp soft brown sugar
3 tbsp creamed coconut
1½ butternut squashes, peeled, seeded and sliced
juice of 1 lime
jasmine rice, to serve

Put the garlic, ginger, chillies, shallots, lime leaves and lemongrass in a food processor or blender and process to make a paste.

Heat the oil in a wok, add the paste and fry for 1-2 minutes. Add the stock and bring to the boil. Reduce the heat and leave to simmer gently for about 10 minutes.

Meanwhile, heat a dry frying pan, add the cashew nuts and toast, stirring, until golden, then set aside.

Stir the fish sauce, sugar and creamed coconut into the mixture in the wok, then add the butternut squash and cook for 8-10 minutes, until just tender. Stir in the cashew nuts with lime juice to taste, then serve with jasmine rice.

NOTES

# Barley risotto with butternut squash

**SERVES 4**

2 butternut squashes, peeled,
seeded and cut into chunks
3 tbsp olive oil
salt and freshly ground black pepper
250g/9oz pearl barley
1 onion, finely chopped
2 cloves garlic, finely chopped
80ml/2½fl oz/⅓ cup white wine
125ml/4fl oz/½ cup vegetable stock
3 tbsp crème fraîche
4 fresh sage leaves, chopped
25g/1oz Parmesan cheese, grated

Preheat the oven to 200°C/400°F/Gas 6. Put the squashes in a roasting tin, drizzle over about half the oil, tossing to coat, and season well with salt and pepper. Roast in the oven for about 30 minutes, turning once or twice during cooking, until tender.

Meanwhile, cook the barley in boiling water for about 25 minutes until tender. Drain and set aside.

Heat the remaining oil in a large pan, add the onion and garlic and fry gently for about 5 minutes, until soft. Stir in the drained barley, pour over the wine and stock, and leave to bubble gently for about 5-10 minutes, stirring occasionally, until most of the liquid has been absorbed.

Stir in the crème fraîche, sage and Parmesan cheese, then fold in the squashes. Season to taste with salt and pepper and serve.

# Chicken tagine with roast squash

**SERVES 4**

2 cloves garlic, crushed
2.5cm/1in piece fresh ginger, peeled
and grated
2 tsp harissa paste
juice of 1 lemon
3 tbsp olive oil, plus extra
for brushing
salt and freshly ground black pepper
1.3kg/3lb chicken
200g/7oz shallots, peeled
2 tsp honey
250ml/9fl oz/1 cup water
1 tsp ground cinnamon
1 butternut squash, about
700g/1lb 9oz in weight, peeled,
seeded and cut into thick slices

Combine the garlic, ginger, harissa, lemon juice and 1 tablespoon of the olive oil and season well with salt and pepper. Pour all over the chicken - inside and out - cover and leave to marinate for at least 1 hour.

Heat the remaining oil in a heavy pan or tagine, add the shallots and cook over a low heat, stirring frequently, for 10 minutes. Add the honey and about 1½ tablespoons of the water and season to taste with salt and pepper. Cook for 5 minutes, until sticky and golden. Push the shallots to the side of the pan and add the chicken. Sprinkle over the cinnamon, pour in the marinating juices and the rest of the water and bring to the boil. Reduce the heat, cover and simmer for 1 hour, turning the chicken occasionally, until cooked through.

Meanwhile, preheat the oven to 200°C/400°F/Gas 6. Twenty minutes before the chicken is ready, put the squash in a baking tin, brush with oil, season well and roast in the oven for 20 minutes.

Remove the chicken from the pan and keep warm. If the sauce is very liquid, boil rapidly for about 5 minutes to thicken. Arrange the squash around the chicken. Pour over the sauce and serve.

# Pumpkin gnocchi with sage butter

**SERVES 4**

250g/9oz prepared pumpkin flesh,
cut into chunks
1 tbsp olive oil
600g/1lb 5oz potatoes, boiled
2 egg yolks
150g/5½oz plain flour
pinch of salt
pinch of freshly grated nutmeg
pinch of ground cinnamon
salt

**FOR THE SAGE BUTTER**

55g/2oz butter
8 fresh sage leaves

Preheat the oven to 200°C/400°F/Gas 6. Put the pumpkin in a baking dish, drizzle over the oil and toss to coat, then bake in the oven for about 20 minutes, until tender. Mash the potatoes and cooked pumpkin together in a large bowl, then press through a sieve and stir in the egg yolks.

Combine the flour, salt, nutmeg and cinnamon in another bowl, then gradually work into the pumpkin mixture to form a soft dough. To form the gnocchi, divide the dough into four, then gently roll each piece into a long sausage, about 1cm/½in in diameter. Cut each length of dough into 2.5cm/1in-long pieces and press each lightly with a fork to make an indent on one side and a ridged pattern on the other. Set aside on a sheet of greaseproof paper.

Make the sage butter. Heat the butter in a pan until sizzling, then add the sage leaves and cook for about 1 minute until the leaves are crisp. Keep warm.

Bring a large pan of salted water to the boil, then add the gnocchi and cook for 2-3 minutes, until they rise to the surface. Scoop them out using a slotted spoon, drain well and serve immediately, drizzled with the sage butter.

## spiced pumpkin soup

To make this wonderfully warming soup, cut a pumpkin, about 1.3kg/3lb in weight, into wedges, scoop out the seeds and arrange in a roasting tin. Drizzle over a few tablespoons of olive oil, season well with salt and freshly ground black pepper and roast in a preheated oven at 200°C/400°F/Gas 6 for about 30 minutes, until tender. Meanwhile, heat another tablespoon of oil in a large pan, add 2 chopped onions and 2 crushed garlic cloves and cook gently until soft. Sprinkle over 1 teaspoon of ground cinnamon and 1 tablespoon of chopped preserved lemon (or, if unavailable, the grated zest of 1 lemon), then pour in about 1.2 litres/2¼ pints/4¾ cups of vegetable or chicken stock and bring to the boil. Reduce the heat and leave to simmer for 10 minutes. Scoop the pumpkin out of its skin and toss into the pan with 2 teaspoons of harissa. Pour into a blender or food processor and process until really smooth. Heat through, check the seasoning and serve.

**NOTES**

# sweet potatoes

Sweet potatoes come into season in autumn and last right through the winter. They may have brown, creamy-yellow or red skins, with flesh varying from pale cream to a deep orange that becomes soft and smooth with a sweet nutty flavour when cooked. Introduced to Europe from the Americas in 1493, and cultivated in southern Spain from the early 16th century, they have had many moments of culinary popularity. They grow best in warmer climates and can be grown successfully in cooler regions only when started off under glass.

When buying, choose smooth-skinned potatoes of an even size and shape. Avoid any that are soft, damaged or beginning to sprout. They keep well if stored in a cool dark place, preferably in an airy basket or similar container. To prepare, scrub them well, then cook in the same way as ordinary potatoes – steam, boil, mash, sauté, roast or deep-fry. When boiled, they are best cooked in their skins, then peeled, to preserve their taste and texture. They are also wonderful baked and stuffed with a piquant filling, such as blue cheese or hot beef chilli and soured cream, to offset their sweet buttery flesh.

## Sweet potato and chicken curry *(opposite)*

**SERVES 4**

2 tbsp sunflower oil
8 green cardamom pods, split open
1 onion, finely chopped
2 cloves garlic, finely chopped
2.5cm/1in piece fresh ginger, peeled and grated
2 green chillies, seeded and chopped
½ tsp ground turmeric
2 tsp ground coriander
400ml/14fl oz/1²⁄₃ cups coconut milk
salt
8 chicken thighs, skinned
750g/1lb 10oz sweet potatoes, peeled and cut into large chunks
juice of 1 lemon
small handful of fresh coriander leaves
rice or Indian breads, to serve

Heat the oil in a pan. Add the cardamom pods and fry over a medium heat for about 2 minutes. Add the onion, garlic, ginger and chillies and fry gently, stirring, for about 5 minutes.

Stir in the turmeric, ground coriander and coconut milk, season to taste with salt and bring to the boil. Add the chicken thighs, pressing them down into the sauce, reduce the heat and leave to simmer for 5 minutes. Stir in the sweet potatoes, cover and continue to simmer for a further 10 minutes.

Uncover the pan, increase the heat slightly and cook for about 10 minutes more, until the chicken is cooked through, the sauce has thickened and the sweet potatoes are tender. Stir once or twice towards the end of the cooking time to prevent the sauce from sticking to the base of the pan. Stir in lemon juice to taste and serve, sprinkled with the fresh coriander leaves and accompanied by rice or Indian breads.

**NOTES**

# citrus fruits

Most citrus fruits thrive in warmer Mediterranean climates, although the tropical lime needs hotter weather to grow successfully. Different citrus fruits come into season at different times of the year, with some, such as Valencia oranges, being available at almost any time and others, such as naval and blood oranges, lemons, limes and grapefruits, being most abundant in autumn and winter.

The sweeter fruits such as oranges, tangerines, clementines, kumquats and grapefruits, along with hybrids, such as ugli fruit and mineolas, can be eaten on their own, while limes and lemons, with their sour juice, work best as flavourings. Citrus segments can be delicious tossed into salads – bittersweet grapefruit is good paired with avocado and crispy bacon, while oranges are delicious with aniseedy fennel or sweet beetroot. Orange juice is a popular additon to many Mediterranean savoury dishes (for example, in pork stews or fish dishes), while lemons and limes feature constantly in marinades. Astringent lemon or lime juice is also used to "pickle" uncooked fish in dishes such as gravadlax and ceviche.

Buy firm fruits that feel heavy for their size, as this indicates plenty of juice. If the rind or zest is needed in a recipe, use unwaxed fruits. Many fruits, such as oranges and clementines, can simply be peeled and eaten as they are. Grapefruit is often halved, the segments cut away from the membranes with a special curved knife and served in their shell. To prepare orange or grapefruit segments without their membranes for a salad, cut a slice off the top and bottom of the fruit to reveal the flesh. Then, with a sharp knife, cut off the skin, with the white pith and membrane, around the whole fruit in strips. Hold the fruit over a bowl to catch any juice, then slice down between the membranes dividing the individual segments to release the flesh.

## zesty lemon curd

This is delicious spread on buttered bread or scones, but is equally good stirred into crème fraîche or whipped cream to make a rich citrus cream. It is also wonderful spooned on to pancakes or used to line the base of fresh-fruit tarts.

To make about 450g/1lb, put the grated rind and juice of 3 large lemons into a large heatproof bowl. Set this over a pan of simmering water, so that the base of the bowl does not touch the water. Add 200g/7oz of caster sugar and stir until the sugar has dissolved. Roughly chop 115g/4oz of unsalted butter into small chunks and stir in until melted. Through a sieve, pour in 3 large beaten eggs and continue cooking, stirring constantly, until the mixture thickens and coats the back of the spoon. Pour into sterilized jars and seal. Leave to cool, then label and store in the fridge. Use within 3 months.

NOTES

# Orange and beetroot salad

**The sharp acidity of oranges makes them the perfect partner for sweet tender beetroot, creating a vibrantly coloured salad that really livens up the autumn table.**

**SERVES 4**
300g/10½oz cooked beetroot
2 oranges
¼ red onion, thinly sliced
25g/1oz walnut halves
2 tsp red-wine vinegar
¼ tsp Dijon mustard
2 tbsp olive oil
salt and freshly ground black pepper

Slice the beetroot and place in a serving bowl. Using a sharp knife, cut a piece from the top and bottom of each orange to reveal the flesh, then, holding it over a clean bowl, cut the peel, with the white pith and membrane around the fruit, off in strips. Slice down the membranes dividing the segments to release the flesh. Discard the peel, pith and membranes and reserve the juice in the bowl. Add the segments to the beetroot, then toss in the onion and walnuts.

Make a dressing by whisking together the reserved orange juice, the vinegar and mustard, then whisk in the oil and season with salt and pepper to taste. Drizzle over the salad, toss gently to combine and serve.

# Pork cooked with orange and white beans

**SERVES 4**
2 tbsp olive oil
1 onion, finely chopped
2 cloves garlic, crushed
500g/1lb 2oz pork loin, trimmed and cubed
100g/3½oz chorizo, cut into small chunks
2 tsp ground cumin
2 tsp ground coriander
grated rind and juice of 1 orange
500g/1lb 2oz tomatoes, peeled (see page 90), seeded and chopped
salt and freshly ground black pepper
400g/14oz can white haricot beans, drained and rinsed
juice of ½ lemon

Heat the oil in a pan, add the onion and garlic and fry gently for about 5 minutes, until soft. Add the pork and chorizo, sprinkle over the ground cumin and coriander and cook, stirring, for about 1-2 minutes.

Add the orange rind and juice and the tomatoes, then season to taste with salt and pepper and stir to mix in. Bring to the boil, lower the heat and leave to simmer gently for about 45 minutes, stirring once or twice, until the sauce becomes thick.

Stir in the drained beans and leave to simmer for a further 10 minutes. Season again with more salt and pepper if necessary, then add lemon juice to taste. Serve.

NOTES

# Orange and ginger steamed pudding

**Infused with the flavours of orange and warming ginger, this indulgent dessert is perfect for bringing a cheering glow to the table during the colder months. To enjoy it to the full, serve with a generous helping of double cream.**

**SERVES 6**

115g/4oz butter, at room temperature
115g/4oz caster sugar
2 eggs
grated rind and juice of 1 orange
3 pieces stem ginger in syrup, chopped
115g/4oz self-raising flour
double cream, to serve

**FOR THE SAUCE**

finely pared rind of 1 orange
55g/2oz caster sugar
2 tbsp syrup from the stem-ginger jar
2 tbsp golden syrup

Grease a 1.2-litre/2¼-pint/4¾-cup pudding basin. Make the sauce by putting the orange rind in a pan of boiling water, lowering the heat and leaving to simmer for about 4 minutes. Drain well, pat dry with kitchen paper and set aside. Put the sugar in a clean pan and heat very gently, stirring, for about 4 minutes, until it melts and turns pale gold. Remove from the heat, then stir in the orange rind, followed by the ginger syrup and golden syrup. Pour the sauce into the greased pudding basin and set aside.

In a large mixing bowl, beat together the butter and sugar until pale and fluffy. Beat in the eggs, one at a time, then stir in the orange rind and juice and the chopped stem ginger. Sift the flour over the top and carefully fold in.

Tip the sponge mixture on top of the sauce in the pudding basin, spreading it out in an even layer. Cover the basin with a double layer of foil and tie it securely in place with string. Put a poaching ring or jam-jar lid in the bottom of a large pan and place the basin on top. Pour water into the pan to come about two-thirds of the way up the side of the basin. Bring the water to the boil, then reduce the heat, cover the pan and leave to simmer gently for about 1½ hours. Check the water level now and again to make sure it is high enough and add more if necessary.

Carefully remove the basin from the pan and leave to rest for about 5 minutes before removing the foil and turning the pudding out on to a serving plate. Serve hot with cream.

# Lemon tart (opposite)

**Few desserts can equal a good lemon tart for indulgence and sophistication. The tang of fresh lemon gives a mouth-puckering lift to the rich creamy sweetness. This version pairs a crisp almond pastry base with a really zesty filling.**

**SERVES 6-8**

200ml/7fl oz/generous ¾ cup crème fraîche
4 eggs
grated rind of 2 lemons
juice of 5 lemons
175g/6oz caster sugar, plus about 2-3 tbsp for the topping

**FOR THE PASTRY**

85g/3oz plain flour
2 tsp caster sugar
40g/1½oz ground almonds
55g/2oz butter, chilled and diced
about 1 tbsp cold water

First make the pastry. Put the flour, sugar and almonds in a food processor and pulse to combine. Add the butter and process until the mixture resembles fine breadcrumbs. With the machine running, add just enough water for the mixture to come together in a ball. Press the pastry together, wrap in clear film and leave in the fridge to chill for at least 30 minutes.

Preheat the oven to 200°C/400°F/Gas 6. Roll out the pastry to line a greased 20cm/8in tart tin, cover with foil and scatter over some baking beans. Bake in the oven for about 10 minutes. Remove the foil and beans and cook for a further 5-10 minutes until the base is crisp. Remove the tart case from the oven and reduce the temperature to 160°C/325°C/Gas 3.

Meanwhile, put the crème fraîche in a bowl and beat in the eggs, one at a time, then stir in the lemon rind and juice and sugar. Pour the mixture into the pastry case, then return it to the oven and bake for 30-35 minutes, until the filling is just set but is still wobbly.

Leave to cool for about 20 minutes, then sprinkle with a thin layer of caster sugar and heat with a kitchen blow-torch until the top is browned and bubbling. Alternatively, cover the pastry with foil and place the tart under a hot grill until the sugar is browned and bubbling.

# grapes

The grape harvest comes at the beginning of autumn, after the long weeks of summer sunshine that are needed to ripen the succulent flesh. The flavour can vary from sugary or tart to the rich scented sweetness of the muscat grape. The skins range in colour from pale yellow through green and red to a dark bluish-black, depending on the variety. Some grapes also have a dusky bloom, while others are waxy.

There are many different types of grape, some grown for eating, others exclusively for making into wine or drying into raisins, sultanas and currants. Many contain tiny seeds, but there are also a number of seedless varieties. Dessert grapes are delicious simply eaten on their own, snipped straight from the bunch using a pair of scissors. However, they can also be paired with a multitude of other ingredients. They have a particular affinity with cheese, so serve alongside a cheeseboard or halved on top of an open cheese sandwhich. They can also be made into juices, sorbets and jellies, used in tarts and cakes and in savoury dishes. Cook them with poultry and feathered game or add to soups.

When buying grapes, the easiest way to check that the fruit is ripe and has a good flavour is to taste a loose fallen grape, if at all possible. Avoid any that are soft, wrinkled, blemished or showing traces of browning or mould. Heavy use of chemicals is frequent in grape cultivation, so it is particularly important to wash the fruits before eating. Rinse them well, then place on a clean cloth to dry. Peeled grapes are often required for use in recipes. To do this, put the grapes in a heatproof bowl, pour over boiling water, then drain almost immediately. The skins should then peel away easily. If the skins still cling to the fruit, repeat the process and try again. To seed grapes, slice in half, then simply pick out the seeds using the point of a sharp knife.

NOTES

# Almond and grape soup

**SERVES 4**
115g/4oz blanched almonds
200g/7oz day-old white bread,
crusts removed
1 clove garlic, chopped
5 tbsp olive oil
200g/7oz whole seedless grapes,
plus a handful, sliced
about 500ml/17fl oz/2 cups
vegetable stock
salt and freshly ground black pepper
1 tbsp sherry vinegar
2 tbsp sherry

Heat a dry frying pan, add the almonds and toast for about 5 minutes until lightly browned. Tip into a food processor or blender and process until finely ground. Leave in the food processor or blender.

Soak the bread in 300ml/10½fl oz/1¼ cups cold water for about 10 minutes, then squeeze dry. Add to the ground almonds, along with the garlic, and process to form a paste.

With the motor running, gradually add the oil and whole grapes, then add enough stock to make a smooth soup. Season to taste with salt and pepper and stir in the vinegar and sherry. Pour into a bowl and chill in the fridge for at least 2 hours. Serve, with the sliced grapes stirred in.

# Rare beef salad with grapes and wasabi dressing

**SERVES 4**
250g/9oz beef sirloin
olive oil, for brushing
juice of 1 lime
¼–½ tsp wasabi paste
2 tbsp sunflower oil
handful of fresh coriander, chopped
salt
115g/4oz mixed salad leaves, such as
lettuce, rocket, baby spinach
and endive
200g/7oz seedless grapes, halved

Trim any fat or sinew from the meat and brush with olive oil. Heat a griddle pan or grill until very hot, then use to cook the meat for about 2 minutes on each side, or to your taste. Lift on to a board, cover with foil and leave to rest for 10 minutes.

Meanwhile, make a dressing by stirring together the lime juice and wasabi paste, then whisking in the sunflower oil and chopped coriander. Season to taste with salt and set aside.

Divide the salad leaves between four serving bowls, then sprinkle the grapes on top. Slice the meat thinly and scatter over the salads. Pour over the dressing, toss to combine and serve.

**NOTES**

# Walnut scones with Brie and grapes

Sweet juicy grapes have a natural affinity with cheese and are fabulous served on top of these savoury scones for afternoon tea or a simple snack. Mild creamy Brie is suggested here, but almost any type of cheese will work well. Try a piquant blue cheese or a sharp mature Cheddar or a crumbly cheese, such as Lancashire or Cheshire.

**MAKES 12**

225g/8oz self-raising flour, plus extra for dusting
1 tsp baking powder
pinch of cayenne pepper
pinch of salt
55g/2oz unsalted butter, chilled and diced
55g/2oz walnut pieces
1 egg, beaten
100ml/3½fl oz/scant ½ cup milk

**TO SERVE**

about 150g/5½oz Brie cheese
about 225g/8oz seedless grapes, sliced

Preheat the oven to 220°C/425°C/Gas 7. Grease a baking sheet.

Combine the flour, baking powder, cayenne pepper and salt in a large bowl. Add the butter and rub into the flour, using your fingertips, until the mixture resembles fine breadcrumbs. Stir in the walnuts and make a well in the centre.

Beat the egg and milk together in a small bowl. Reserving about 1½ tablespoons of the mixture, pour the remainder into the well in the flour mixture and gradually bring together using a fork to form a soft dough. Add extra milk, if necessary. Turn on to a lightly floured surface and knead very briefly, then roll out to about 2.5cm/1in thick. Using a 5cm/2in biscuit cutter, cut the dough into 12 rounds. Arrange on the baking sheet, spacing them slightly apart. Brush the tops with the reserved milk and egg mixture and bake for about 10 minutes, until risen and golden. Transfer to a wire rack to cool.

To serve, split the cooled scones in half and top each half with a slice of Brie and a scattering of sliced grapes.

## grape jelly

Grape jelly is delicious spread on toast. This version is scented with cardamom, but fresh ginger or elderflower cordial both work well too. Put 900g/2lb of grapes in a pan with the juice and pips of 2 lemons and the crushed seeds of about 10 cardamom pods. Bring to the boil, reduce the heat, cover and simmer for about 1½ hours. Mash the grapes with a potato masher, then pour the mixture into a scalded jelly bag suspended over a large glass bowl and leave to drain overnight. Never squeeze the bag as this will give cloudy results. Measure the juice collected into a clean pan and add 450g/1lb of sugar for every 600ml/1 pint/2½ cups of grape juice. Heat gently, stirring, until the sugar has dissolved, then bring to the boil and cook until the jelly reaches 105°C/220°F. Skim off any scum, then ladle into sterilized jars and cover, seal and label. Store in a cool, dark place.

# figs

The appearance of figs marks the closing days of summer and the start of autumn. Figs thrive in warm climates and have been cultivated in the Mediterranean and Middle East for millennia. Depending on variety, they may have green, amber or purplish-black skin, the tender insides being made up almost entirely of tiny dark seeds, surrounded by pink, amber, violet and red flesh.

When figs are really fresh and ripe, they are wonderful eaten just as they are. Simply cut in half and scoop out the moreish flesh with a teaspoon. They are also delicious cut into wedges and tossed into salads, or try scooping fresh fig flesh on top of Parma ham or blue cheese in a sandwich instead of a classic chutney. Figs are also good cooked – in fruit compotes or a sweet syrup, in tarts, in jams and preserves and dished up with game or poultry.

When choosing figs, look for plump, unblemished fruits that give slightly when gently squeezed. They need little preparation apart from washing. Cut or slice them lengthways so that you can still appreciate the shape of the whole fruit. Raw figs are best eaten warm, never cold or chilled. If you can, place them on a sunny windowsill for an hour or so before serving.

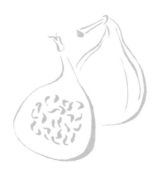

## baked figs with honey and crème fraîche

One of the best and simplest ways to eat figs is to bake them with honey and crème fraîche to make a glorious melt-in-the-mouth dessert. Allow about 3 figs per person. Trim off the woody tip of each fig and cut halfway down each one into quarters, then gently press the bottom so that the quarters splay out. Arrange the figs in a baking dish, spoon about a tablespoon of crème fraîche into each one, then drizzle a little honey on top. Bake in a preheated oven at 220°C/425°F/Gas 7 for 5–10 minutes until golden and bubbling. Serve immediately with the syrupy juices spooned over.

**NOTES**

# Guinea fowl cooked with figs and red wine

**SERVES 6**

2 guinea fowl, about
1kg/2lb 4oz each
salt and freshly ground black pepper
3 tbsp olive oil
8 figs, halved
large handful of fresh thyme
250ml/9fl oz/1 cup red wine
250ml/9fl oz/1 cup chicken stock
1 tbsp flour

Preheat the oven to 180°C/350°F/Gas 4. Season the birds all over with plenty of salt and pepper. Heat 2 tbsp of the oil in a large frying pan, add the birds and brown on all sides. Transfer to a baking dish or roasting tin.

Arrange the figs around the birds, tuck in the sprigs of thyme and pour over the wine and stock. Roast in the oven for about 1 hour, until the juices run clear when the thickest part of the thigh is pierced with a knife or skewer.

Remove the birds and figs from the dish, cover with foil and keep warm. Discard the thyme. Heat the remaining oil in a pan and stir in the flour. Cook for about 1 minute, then stir in the cooking juices and heat gently until thickened to a rich gravy. Transfer to a jug or gravy boat and serve with the guinea fowl and figs.

# Fig and goat's cheese salad

**SERVES 4**

1 tbsp balsamic vinegar
2 tbsp olive oil
salt and freshly ground black pepper
1½ tbsp pinenuts
about 175g/6oz salad leaves, such
as lettuce, rocket, baby spinach
and endive
4 figs, cut into wedges
8 slices of a baguette
200g/7oz goat's cheese, cut into
8 slices
2 tsp clear honey

Make a dressing by whisking together the vinegar and oil in a small bowl. Season to taste with salt and pepper and set aside.

Heat a dry frying pan, add the pinenuts and cook, stirring, for about 3 minutes until golden. Set aside. Divide the salad leaves between four serving plates and scatter the fig wedges on top.

Preheat the grill until hot and use to toast the bread on one side until golden. Turn over, place a slice of cheese on each piece of bread, then drizzle with honey and a grinding of black pepper. Grill for 2-3 minutes, until golden and bubbling.

Drizzle the dressing over each salad, top each with two cheesy toasts, sprinkle with the pinenuts and serve immediately.

**NOTES**

# Roast fig tartlets

**These simple-to-make little tartlets are fabulous eaten warm or at room temperature. The subtle combination of crisp almond pastry, mild vanilla custard and sweet, fragrant figs is absolutely irresistible. You will find it hard to stop at just one.**

**MAKES 12**
80ml/2½fl oz/⅓ cup crème fraîche
1 egg yolk
¼ tsp vanilla extract
½ tbsp icing sugar
6 figs
½-1 tbsp clear honey

**FOR THE PASTRY**
3 tbsp ground almonds
100g/3½oz plain flour
1 tbsp caster sugar
55g/2oz butter, chilled and diced
2 tbsp water

First make the pastry. Put the almonds, flour and sugar in a food processor and pulse to combine. Add the butter and pulse until the mixture resembles fine breadcrumbs. With the motor running, gradually add the water until the mixture comes together in a ball. Wrap in clear film and chill in the fridge for at least 30 minutes.

Preheat the oven to 190°C/375°F/Gas 5 and grease a 12-hole tartlet tin. Roll out the pastry thinly. Cut out 12 rounds, using a 7.5cm/3in round biscuit cutter. Press the rounds into the tartlet tin and prick the bases with a fork. Bake for about 10 minutes in the oven until crisp and lightly golden.

Meanwhile, beat together the crème fraîche, egg yolk, vanilla extract and icing sugar in a bowl and set aside. Cut off the woody tip from the stem of each fig, then cut the fruits in half lengthways.

Remove the tartlet cases from the oven and put a tablespoon of the crème fraîche mixture in the bottom of each. Nestle a fig half on top and add a little more of crème fraîche mixture if room. Drizzle with honey and bake in the oven for about 10 minutes, until the figs are tender and the custard is just turning golden. Remove to a wire rack to cool slightly before serving.

## cheese, ham and fig croissant

Figs, partnered with melting cheese and Parma ham, make a sublime filling for a toasted croissant. Halve the croissant and top the bottom half with a slice of Gruyère cheese. Lightly toast both halves until the cheese on one is melting and the other is golden. Top the cheesy half with a couple of slices of Parma ham and a few scoops of flesh from a ripe fig. Grind over some black pepper, place the toasted half-croissant on top and enjoy.

# pomegranates

Native to Iran, pomegranates thrive in hot sunny climates. They arrive on our tables in late autumn. Round, tapering to an elegant, chimney-like stem, these leathery-skinned fruit are tightly packed with glistening, jewel-like, red seeds, each rich with an intensely flavoured sweet-sour juice, which can be used in both sweet and savoury dishes – much in the same way that lemon juice is. This juice is particularly popular in Persian cuisine and is also made into a sweet concentrated syrup called grenadine, that can be added to cocktails and be diluted with water to make a refreshing drink. As they are so attractive, the whole seeds are frequently sprinkled over dishes as a garnish.

When buying pomegranates, choose fruit that feel heavy for their size, as this indicates that they contain plenty of juice. To remove the seeds, cut the fruit into quarters and, holding each piece over a bowl, sharply tap the back with a wooden spoon. The seeds should pop out unscathed into the bowl and can then be used whole or pressed in a sieve to extract the juice.

## Pan-fried duck with pomegranate sauce (opposite)

**SERVES 4**
4 ripe pomegranates
4 duck breasts, about 200g/7oz each
salt and freshly ground black pepper
2 cloves garlic, crushed
1 tbsp flour
125ml/4fl oz/½ cup chicken or duck stock

Cut the pomegranates into quarters, hold each piece over a bowl and tap the back sharply with a wooden spoon, so that the seeds pop out. Set about a quarter of them aside. Put the rest in a sieve over a clean bowl and press with the back of a spoon to release the juice.

Score the skin of the duck in a lattice pattern and rub with plenty of salt and pepper. Heat a non-stick frying pan and place the duck, skin-side down, into the pan. Cook for 10 minutes over a medium heat. Pour away most of the fat, turn over the duck and cook for another 4–5 minutes. Remove from the pan, set aside and keep warm.

Add the garlic to the pan and stir for about 30 seconds, stir in the flour and cook, stirring, for 1 minute. Gradually stir in the pomegranate juice and stock and cook for 2–3 minutes, until the sauce has thickened. Season to taste with salt and pepper, then stir in the reserved pomegranate seeds. Serve with the duck.

NOTES

# plums

Glorious fat plums with their bluish bloom help welcome in the autumn. There are hundreds of different varieties – including damsons and greengages – and their skin-colour ranges from dark purple to red, green and yellow. All have fragrant juicy flesh, that can vary from pinkish red to golden amber. Dessert plums can be eaten raw or cooked – baked, poached or even pan-fried with sugar, or in pies and cakes. Cooking plums are tarter with a drier flesh and are good for poaching, baking and making into jam. Golden-skinned greengages have a honeyed taste and are particularly good eaten raw, while blue-black damsons have an intense tart flavour, making them better suited to cooking.

When buying, look for firm, unblemished fruits. A good blue-purplish bloom indicates that they have not been overhandled. Plums should be eaten within a few days, as they become too soft and over-ripe very quickly.

Plums may be cooked with the stone in or out. To remove it, cut around the plum along its natural crease, then gently twist the two sides apart and prise out the stone. When making a purée, simply cook the plums whole, then sieve out the stones and skin. When making jam, just skim the stones off the surface during cooking.

If skinned plums are asked for in a recipe, cut a cross in the base of each fruit, place in a heatproof bowl and pour over boiling water. Leave them to stand for about 30 seconds, then drain. The skins should peel away easily.

## oven-poached plums

Plums are wonderful poached, then served hot or cold with plenty of cream or crème fraîche. To prepare, preheat the oven to 150°C/300°F/Gas 2. Arrange 500g/1lb 2oz plums, halved and stoned, in a single layer in a large baking dish. Sprinkle over a little ground cinnamon and 1 tablespoon of caster sugar. Tuck in 3 whole cloves around the fruit, pour over the juice of 1 orange and 1 tablespoon of brandy, then bake in the oven for about 30 minutes, spooning the juices over the plums once or twice during cooking.

**NOTES**

# Plum and marzipan tarte tatin

**The classic *tarte tatin* is made with apples. This version, however – made with marzipan-stuffed plums – makes a wonderful alternative. You can also use the basic recipe for an apple or pear tart if you wish: just peel, halve and core the fruit, toss in lemon juice, and cook as described below, omitting the marzipan.**

**SERVES 6-8**

400g/14oz puff pastry
flour, for dusting
100g/3½oz marzipan
55g/2oz butter
55g/2oz sugar
600g/1lb 5oz plums, halved and stoned
crème fraîche, to serve

Preheat the oven to 200°C/400°F/Gas 6. Roll out the pastry on a lightly floured surface and, using a 23cm/9in *tarte tatin* tin as a guide, cut out a large round. Roll up, wrap in clear film and set aside in the refrigerator.

Divide the marzipan into 16-20 pieces (according the number of plum halves you have), roll into balls and flatten slightly so that they will fit into the plums. Set aside.

Melt the butter in the *tarte tatin* tin (or in a cast iron frying pan with an ovenproof handle) and sprinkle over the sugar. Allow to bubble for 1-2 minutes, then arrange the plums, cut-side up, in a single layer in the tin and continue to bubble for a further 8-9 minutes, until the syrup is dark and caramely.

Remove the tin from the heat and place a flattened ball of marzipan in the centre of each plum half. Place the round of pastry over the top of the fruit, tucking the edges down around the plums. Bake in the oven for 25-30 minutes until the pastry is puffed up and golden.

Leave the tart to cool for about 10 minutes, then place a serving plate over the top of the tin and flip it over to tip the tart out of the tin on to the plate, with the fruit on top. If necessary, rearrange the fruit slightly. Serve warm or at room temperature with a generous helping of crème fraîche.

**NOTES**

# apples

There are thousands of different varieties of apple, coming into season at different times. Many keep well, so apples are usually available from cold-storage and can be enjoyed for most of the year. Early-cropping apples, however - coming in at the end of summer and beginning of autumn - tend not to store well, so should be taken advantage of while in season.

As a general rule, apples can be split into two groups: "eating" and "cooking". Eating apples are sweet and good eaten raw, although they may be cooked, while cooking apples are sour and are usually prepared with sugar.

Choose firm, unblemished apples and avoid those that are wrinkled or bruised. Remember that skin-colour is no indication of flavour. To prepare for cooking, simply peel and core. Apple flesh quickly turns brown when exposed to air so, unless using the fruit immediately, toss cut apples in lemon juice to preserve its crisp creamy colour.

Apples are delicious cooked in tarts, pies, cakes and other desserts and go well with warm spices such as cinnamon, ginger and cloves. Stew them in a splash of water with a couple of whole cloves, or bake them in a crumble. Cooking apples can be cored, then stuffed with sugar, dried fruit and butter and baked until tender, or turned into a sharp sauce to serve with pork.

## Spicy pork chops with caramelized apples

**SERVES 4**

2 Bramley apples
25g/1oz butter
1 tsp soft brown sugar
2 tsp balsamic vinegar
salt and freshly ground black pepper
1 tbsp olive oil
4 pork loin steaks, about 200g/7oz each
4 tbsp sherry
6 juniper berries, crushed

Peel, core and quarter the apples. Melt the butter in a frying pan, add the prepared apples and fry for about 3 minutes, turning to cook all over. Sprinkle over the sugar and vinegar and season to taste with salt and pepper. Cook, turning occasionally, for about 5 minutes, until caramelized and sticky. Set aside.

Heat the oil in a clean frying pan, add the pork steaks and cook for about 3 minutes on each side, until well browned. Add the sherry, juniper berries and caramelized apples. Season to taste with more salt and pepper, if needed, and bubble gently for about 5-6 minutes, until the pork is cooked through. Serve.

**NOTES**

# Apple strudel

**SERVES 6-8**
1 tsp ground cinnamon
1 tbsp soft brown sugar
55g/2oz blanched almonds
55g/2oz sultanas
2 large eating apples
12 sheets filo pastry
melted butter, for brushing
icing sugar, for dusting

Preheat the oven to 190°C/375°F/Gas 5. Grease a baking sheet.

Combine the cinnamon and sugar in a large bowl and set aside. Heat a dry frying pan, add the almonds and toast for 3 minutes, stirring, until golden. Roughly chop, and add to the sugar and cinnamon mixture with the sultanas. Peel, core and slice the apples, then add to the mixture and toss together to combine.

Lay one sheet of filo pastry on a board, brush with melted butter, then lay another sheet next to it, overlapping slightly, and again brush it with melted butter. Add a third overlapping sheet to make a large rectangle and brush that with butter. Lay another three sheets on top, arranging and buttering them in the same way. Repeat with the remaining filo sheets until there are four layers of pastry.

Spread the apple mixture down the centre of the pastry, leaving space at either end. Tuck the short ends of the pastry over the apple filling, then roll up into a log. Carefully lift on to the baking sheet, tucking the folded ends underneath. Brush with more melted butter, then bake in the oven for about 35 minutes, until crisp and golden. Serve warm or cold, dusted with icing sugar.

# Brandied baked apples

**SERVES 4**
4 Bramley apples
55g/2oz butter, at room temperature
2 tbsp brown sugar
handful of ready-to-eat dried figs, finely chopped
handful of ready-to-eat dried apricots, finely chopped
1 tsp ground cinnamon
juice of 2 oranges
5 tbsp brandy
thick cream, to serve

Preheat the oven to 190°C/375°F/Gas 5. Core the apples, leaving them whole, and place in a baking dish.

Cream together the butter and brown sugar, then stir in the dried figs and apricots and the cinnamon. Using a teaspoon, fill the cored apples with the mixture.

Pour the orange juice and brandy over the apples, cover the dish with foil and bake in the oven for 35 minutes. Remove the foil and cook for about 15 minutes more, until the apples are tender. Serve with the juices drizzled over the top and a generous helping of thick cream.

**NOTES**

# Apple and blackberry crumble

**SERVES 4-6**
4 eating apples
150g/5½oz blackberries
2 tsp ground cinnamon
thick cream or custard, to serve

**FOR THE CRUMBLE**
115g/4oz flour
115g/4oz chilled butter, chopped
55g/2oz soft brown sugar
100g/3½oz hazelnuts, toasted and
roughly chopped

Preheat the oven to 190°C/375°F/Gas 5. First make the crumble. Put the flour, butter and sugar in a food processor and process until the mixture resembles fine breadcrumbs. Tip into a bowl, stir in the hazelnuts and set aside.

Peel, core and slice the apples, then scatter layers of apple and blackberries in a baking dish, sprinkling cinnamon between the layers.

Top with the crumble mixture in an even layer, then bake in the oven for about 50 minutes until the fruit is tender and bubbling and the crumble topping golden. Serve with thick cream or custard.

# Sour cream apple cake

**MAKES 1 x 20CM/8IN CAKE**
85g/3oz butter
2 Bramley apples, peeled, cored
and sliced
6 tbsp crème fraîche
grated rind and juice of 1 lemon
150g/5½oz sugar
1½ tbsp plain flour
6 eggs, separated

**FOR THE FILLING**
325ml/11fl oz/1⅓ cups
crème fraîche
½ tsp vanilla essence
4 tsp caster sugar

**FOR THE TOPPING**
1 tbsp caster sugar
1½ tsp ground cinnamon
2 tbsp slivered almonds

Preheat the oven to 170°C/325°F/Gas 3. Line the base of three 20cm/8in-diameter, shallow, loose-based, round cake tins.

Melt the butter in a pan, add the apples and cook gently for about 8 minutes, stirring, until pulpy. Beat together the crème fraîche, lemon rind and juice, sugar, flour and egg yolks and stir into the apples. Heat gently, stirring, for about 5 minutes, until the mixture thickens. Set aside. Combine the topping ingredients in a bowl and set aside.

In a clean bowl, whisk the egg whites until they form stiff peaks. Carefully fold, a few tablespoons at a time, into the apple mixture. Divide among the lined tins and spread out evenly. Scatter the prepared topping over one of the cakes, then bake all three in the oven for about 45 minutes, until firm and golden. Leave to cool in the tins, then carefully turn out and peel off the lining paper. Cover with clear film and leave in the fridge to chill.

Meanwhile, combine the filling ingredients in another clean bowl. Spread half on top of one of the plain cake rounds, top with the second plain round and the remaining cream, and place the cinnamon-and-almond-topped cake round on top. Slice and serve.

# pears

Harvested in late summer and autumn and available from cold-storage well into spring, pears are a boon during the colder months, when other fresh fruit is generally unavailable. These fragrant honeyed fruits come in a great variety of flavours, textures and colours. Some have crisp white flesh, while others have a meltingly soft, almost grainy texture. They can be eaten raw or sliced and tossed into salads, and are particularly good combined with sharp-flavoured cheeses. They are also delicious cooked - poached, pan-fried, in tarts and cakes and with meat or game.

Pears should be picked and sold before they are fully ripe. When buying, look for firm fruits that you can take home to ripen. A pear will be yielding to the touch around the stem when ripe, but not soft. Really firm varieties, such as the conference pear, are often the best for cooking.

Eaten raw, pears may be peeled or eaten with their skins on. Many cooked recipes require them to be peeled, which can be done simply with a vegetable peeler. The core is much smaller and tenderer than the apple core, and can be cut away easily if the fruit is quartered or cut into wedges. Halved pears can be cored using a melon baller, but to remove the core while leaving the pear whole - as may be required for poached pears - it is easiest to use a pointed apple corer or long vegetable peeler.

## poached pears

Pears are delicious poached in a lightly spiced syrup and served hot or cold with cream or ice cream. This version uses white wine and fragrant star anise, but red wine and warm spices, such as cinnamon, work just as well. Peel 4 pears and remove the cores with an apple corer or long pointed vegetable peeler, leaving the fruits whole. Gently heat 500ml/17fl oz/2 cups of white wine and 2 tablespoons of granulated sugar in a pan, stirring, until the sugar has dissolved. Add the pears and 1 star anise and bring to the boil. Reduce the heat, cover and simmer for 25-30 minutes, turning the pears once or twice, until tender. Transfer the pears to a dish, then increase the heat and boil the syrup for about 15 minutes until reduced and thickened. Pour over the pears and serve hot or cold.

NOTES

# Chocolate crêpes with caramelized pears

**Pears and chocolate have a natural affinity. This is the perfect dessert to serve as a treat, when the nights are drawing in and the temperature is starting to drop.**

**SERVES 4**
125ml/4fl oz/½ cup single cream
55g/2oz dark chocolate
1 tbsp golden syrup
1 tbsp brandy
25g/1oz butter
4 pears, peeled, cored and cut into wedges

**FOR THE CRÊPES**
115g/4oz plain flour
pinch of salt
2 eggs, beaten
300ml/10½fl oz/1¼ cups milk
butter, for frying

First make the crêpes. Sift the flour and salt into a bowl and make a well in the middle. Pour the beaten eggs and half the milk into the well and gradually mix in the flour to make a smooth batter. Whisk in the rest of the milk, then leave to stand for 20 minutes.

Heat a crêpe pan until very hot, then add a little butter and wipe over the surface with a piece of kitchen paper to leave a thin film. Add a small ladleful of batter to the pan, tipping it so that a thin even layer covers the base. Cook for about 1 minute, until golden underneath, then flip over and cook the other side for about 30 seconds, until golden. Slide on to a plate. Cook another seven crêpes in the same way, layering them between sheets of kitchen paper. Set aside and keep warm.

Put the cream, chocolate, syrup and brandy in a pan and heat gently, stirring, until melted and combined. Set aside and keep warm.

Heat the butter in a frying pan, add the pears and fry on both sides until golden. Fold each crêpe into four to make a cone, fill with pears, drizzle with the chocolate sauce and serve.

## pear and blue cheese crostini

Ripe, juicy pears and blue cheese are great partners. Served together on little toasts, they make a superb accompaniment to pre-dinner drinks. Cut a small baguette into thick slices. Brush lightly with olive oil, then toast on both sides until golden. While still warm, top with a slither of Gorgonzola cheese and a small wedge of ripe pear. Serve immediately.

# quinces

A frequently underrated autumn treat, the quince, a relative of the apple and pear, has a heady aroma and sharp citrusy flavour. It is said that quinces are at their best grown in cold climates so that they ripen very slowly, giving their intense fragrance and flavour time to develop. In unripe fruits, the yellow skin is covered with a downy coating, but this disappears as the fruit ripens, leaving a smooth skin like that of a pear.

Quinces are too tart to eat raw, so should always be cooked, usually with plenty of sugar. They are wonderful turned into a clear jelly and are the key ingredient in the coarse Spanish fruit "cheese" *membrillo*, which is traditionally served with slices of Manchego cheese as a tapas dish to accompany drinks. The Portuguese call the quince *marmelada*, revealing the heritage of the sticky orange marmalade that we know today, which was originally made with quinces. They are also wonderful cooked with poultry and game, and a quince sauce makes an excellent accompaniment to pork.

Quinces are more likely to found growing in private gardens than for sale on a greengrocer's stall, but they are well worth trying if you get the opportunity. Look for ripe yellow fruits. Be warned, though –as they tend to rot from the inside, even a fruit that looks blemish-free may be revealed as being no good when cut open.

To prepare, wash, then peel using a vegetable peeler. The fruit is surprisingly hard, so carefully cut into quarters using a sharp heavy knife and remove the core. Like that of apples and pears, the flesh browns when exposed to air. However, this is not a problem, as quince flesh turns a deep pinkish-amber when cooked and any previous dicolouration will go unnoticed.

Autumn

## baked quinces

This delicious dessert can be put together in a matter of minutes, then left to bake while the main course is eaten.

To prepare, beat together 85g/3oz of butter, 40g/1½oz of brown sugar and 2 teaspoons of ground cinnamon in a bowl until creamy. Halve 4 quinces, remove and discard the cores and arrange in an ovenproof dish. Spread the cinnamon mixture on top and bake in a preheated oven at 190°C/375°F/Gas 5 for about 30 minutes, until tender. Serve.

NOTES

# Roast duck breasts with quinces

**Fragrant roast quinces are the perfect foil for the robust taste of tender juicy duck. The combination of honeyed quince and richly flavoured duck in every mouthful is heavenly.**

**SERVES 4**

4 duck breasts, about
200g/7oz each
salt and freshly ground black pepper
1 tbsp olive oil
3 quinces, peeled, cored
and quartered
2 tsp clear honey
juice of 1 lemon
1 tbsp flour
2 tbsp sherry
240ml/8fl oz/scant 1 cup
chicken stock

Preheat the oven to 220°C/425°F/Gas 7.

Score the duck skin in a lattice pattern and season well with salt and pepper. Place the duck, skin-side up, in a roasting tin and spinkle over the olive oil.

Place the quinces in a bowl. Combine the honey and half the lemon juice in a jug, pour over the quinces and toss to coat. Nestle them around the duck and roast in the oven for about 20 minutes until the duck is cooked and the quinces tender.

Remove the duck and quinces to a serving dish, cover with foil and keep warm. Make a gravy by pouring off all but 1-2 tablespoons of fat from the roasting tin, then place it over a low heat. Stir in the flour and cook for about 1 minute. Gradually stir in the sherry and stock and simmer for about 2 minutes until thickened. Remove from the heat, season to taste with salt and pepper and the remaining lemon juice, then serve with the duck and quinces.

## membrillo

This thick quince jelly is a speciality of Spain, traditionally served in slices with Manchego cheese. The sweetness of the *membrillo* is a perfect foil for the saltiness of the cheese. To make, line a rectangular dish or roasting tin with greaseproof paper. Put 900g/2lb of peeled and chopped quinces in a large pan and pour over enough water to cover. Bring to the boil, reduce the heat and simmer until the fruit is soft. Drain well, then mash the fruit and press through a seive to achieve a fine purée. Weigh the purée and put into a clean pan with an equal weight of sugar. Heat gently, stirring continuously, until the purée turns a deep red colour. Pour into the lined dish or tin to a depth of about 2.5cm/1in and leave to cool.

# hedgerow fruits

Picking wild fruits from hedgerows is one of the best autumn activities. A pail of freshly gathered blackberries can be made into a fruity crumble, and hard bitter sloes can be dropped into gin to make a fragrant, ruby-red spirit, that is perfect for serving at Christmas. Rosehips, crab apples and elderberries are all good for making into jelly.

The shiny globular blackberry – or bramble, as it is also known – is probably the most widely harvested and used of all hedgerow fruits. It grows wild, but bushes are also cultivated. On their own, blackberries can have a slightly bland flavour, so are frequently paired with other fruits such as apples. They do not keep well, and should be eaten within a day of picking or buying; discard any that are mushy. Blackberries do freeze well, however, and can be frozen in a single layer on a lined baking sheet, then transferred to a sealed bag or container and returned to the freezer for later use. As well as being good in fruit crumbles, blackberries are also delicious turned into preserves and cooked with other hedgerow fruits, such as tiny black elderberries.

Rosehips are the fruits of the wild rose. They are mainly used to make a syrup, which can be diluted with water to make a fragrant drink, or used to flavour milky desserts such as rice pudding or ice cream, or be made into jelly.

Tiny black sloes are a type of wild plum that grow widely in hedgerows throughout Europe. The raw fruit is mouth-puckeringly sour and bitter – but infused in gin, the flavour mellows, producing a delicious ruby-coloured drink. Freezing is also said to mellow the flavour, so it may be worth freezing any picked before the first frosts for a couple of days before using.

## sloe gin

To make sloe gin, wash and remove the stems from 450g/1lb of sloes and prick the fruits all over using a toothpick. Put in a large Kilner jar, sprinkle over 225g/8oz of caster sugar and pour over about 1 litre/1¾ pints/4 cups of gin. Seal the jar and keep in a cool place. Shake every day for one week, then once a week for the next 2 months. At this stage, the liqueur is ready to drink but its flavour will improve with keeping, so, if you can, strain into bottles and leave to mature for at least 6 months before drinking.

NOTES

# Blackberry and elderberry jelly

**MAKES ABOUT 900G/2LB**
900g/2lb blackberries
225g/8oz elderberries, stalks
removed
pips from 2 lemons
granulated sugar (see recipe)

Wash and pick over the fruit, discarding any over-ripe or mushy berries. Put into a large pan with the lemon pips. Pour over just enough water to cover, bring to the boil, then reduce the heat, cover and leave to simmer gently for about 1 hour.

Remove from the heat, mash the fruit well with a potato masher and leave to cool. Pour the mixture into a scalded jelly bag suspended over a large bowl and leave to drain overnight.

Measure the strained juice in the bowl and pour into a large pan. Add 450g/1lb sugar for every 600ml/1 pint/2½ cups juice, then heat gently, stirring, until the sugar has dissolved. Turn up the heat and allow to boil rapidly until the temperature reaches 105°C/220°F (test with a sugar thermometer). Remove from the heat, skim off any scum and ladle the jelly into sterilized jars. Seal and leave to cool before labelling and storing in a cool dark place.

# Rosehip syrup

**MAKES ABOUT 2.5 LITRES/**
**4½ PINTS/10 CUPS**
900g/2lb rosehips
2.5 litres/4½ pints/10 cups
cold water
450g/1lb granulated sugar

Wash and pick over the rosehips, discarding any that are brown and mushy. Put in a blender or food processor and process until roughly chopped. Put in a pan, pour over 1.75 litres/3 pints/7 cups of the water and bring to the boil. Remove from the heat and leave to stand for 15 minutes, then pour into a jelly bag suspended over a large bowl and leave to drain overnight.

Return the pulp in the jelly bag to the pan, pour over the remaining water and bring to the boil. Leave to stand for about 15 minutes, then drain through the jelly bag into the bowl.

Pour all the juice into a clean pan, add the sugar and heat gently, stirring, until the sugar has dissolved. Bring to the boil and boil rapidly until the mixture has reduced to about 850ml/1½ pints/3½ cups. Pour the syrup into bottles, label and store.

# game

Game is traditionally associated with the colder months of the year and is in abundance during autumn and winter. Much game, such as rabbit, venison, quail and duck, is now farmed, so is readily available outside the wild season, but some, such as hare and woodcock, is not and remains a seasonal treat. Wild game, however, is often considered to have by far the better flavour.

Game can be divided into two categories – furred and feathered. The furred variety includes boar, venison, rabbit and hare, while the feathered includes all the game birds from pheasant, quail and duck to woodcock, partridge, grouse and pigeon.

Some people believe that to get the freshest and tastiest game they need to buy it still feathered or furred and pluck, skin and gut it themselves. However, for those that do not relish the idea of doing this, there are plenty of good butchers and game dealers where it can be bought ready-prepared. Most game should be hung for several days after killing in order to develop the flavour, but generally the butcher or game dealer will do this too, both for game sold ready for cooking and for game that still needs preparing for the pot.

## Venison sausages with sweet potato mash

**SERVES 4**
2 tbsp olive oil
8–12 venison sausages
2 onions, halved and sliced
2 cloves garlic, sliced
1 tbsp soft brown sugar
250ml/9fl oz/1 cup red wine
salt and freshly ground black pepper
3 sprigs of fresh thyme or ¼ tsp dried thyme

**FOR THE MASH**
1kg/2lb 4oz sweet potatoes, peeled and cut into large chunks
salt
85g/3oz butter
2 red chillies, seeded and finely chopped

Preheat the oven to 190°C/375°F/Gas 5. Heat the oil in a large frying pan. Prick the sausages, add to the pan and brown all over. Transfer to a baking dish and arrange in a single layer.

Toss the onions and garlic into the frying pan and cook gently, stirring occasionally, for about 10 minutes. Sprinkle over the sugar and cook, stirring, for a further 5 minutes. Pour over the wine, season to taste with salt and pepper, add the dried thyme, if using, and bring to the boil. Pour the mixture over the sausages, tuck in the fresh thyme, if using, cover the dish with foil and bake in the oven for about 30 minutes.

About 15 minutes before the end of the cooking time, prepare the mash. Cook the sweet potatoes in boiling salted water for 10–15 minutes until tender, drain well and mash. Melt the butter in a pan, add the chilli and fry for 1–2 minutes, then stir into the potatoes. Serve with the sausages and onion gravy.

**NOTES**

# Spiced braised duck with pears

**SERVES 4**

4 duck legs
salt and freshly ground black pepper
2 tbsp olive oil
2 cloves garlic, crushed
400ml/14fl oz/1⅔ cups chicken stock
1 tsp ground ginger
2 tsp ground cinnamon
½ tsp smoked paprika
2 pears, cored, peeled and quartered
1 tbsp soft brown sugar

Preheat the oven to 180°C/350°F/Gas 4. Season the duck legs with salt and pepper, then heat half the oil in a large frying pan. Add the duck and fry for about 5 minutes until well browned. Transfer to an ovenproof dish and arrange in a single layer. Drain most of the fat from the pan, add the garlic and gently fry for 1 minute. Stir in the stock, ginger, cinnamon and paprika, bring to the boil, then pour over the duck. Bake in the oven for 1¼ hours.

About 10 minutes before the end of the cooking time, heat the remaining oil in a clean pan, add the pears and fry for 5 minutes, until golden. Sprinkle over the sugar and cook for 4–5 minutes. Add to the duck in the casserole and cook for 15 minutes, until the duck is cooked and the pears tender.

Transfer the duck and pears to a serving dish and keep warm. Skim the fat off the cooking juices, season with salt and pepper if needed, pour over the duck and pears and serve.

# North African-style pigeon pie

**SERVES 6**

3 pigeons, oven-ready
90g/3¼oz butter
1 onion, chopped
1 cinnamon stick
½ tsp ground ginger
1 tsp paprika
1 tsp ground coriander
handful of fresh flat-leaf parsley, chopped
6 eggs, beaten
salt and freshly ground black pepper
100g/3½oz almonds, toasted and roughly chopped
115g/4oz dried apricots, finely chopped
1 tsp ground cinnamon, plus extra for dusting
12 sheets filo pastry

Put the pigeons in a large pan with 25g/1oz of the butter, the onion, spices (except for the ground cinnamon) and parsley. Pour over enough water to cover and bring to the boil. Reduce the heat, cover and simmer for 1 hour. Transfer the birds to a board and strain and reserve the stock. Skin and bone the birds, chop the flesh into bite-size pieces and set aside. Pour 150ml/5fl oz/⅔ cup of the stock into a clean pan and stir in the eggs. Heat gently, stirring, for about 25 minutes to form a thick sauce. Season well with salt and pepper. Preheat the oven to 190°C/375°F/Gas 5.

Melt the remaining butter in a pan, and use to brush the inside of a baking dish. Line the dish with 6 sheets of filo pastry, brushing each sheet with butter and leaving any long pieces overhanging the dish. Spread over half the pigeon meat, then sprinkle with half the almonds, apricots and ground cinnamon and half the sauce. Top with the remaining pigeon, almonds, apricots, ground cinnamon and sauce. Fold over the overhanging pastry, then top with the remaining filo, again brushing each sheet with butter. Bake in the oven for 45 minutes. Serve hot or warm, dusted with extra ground cinnamon.

# Roast quail with sage and bacon (opposite)

**SERVES 4**
2 tbsp olive oil
juice of 1 lemon
1 tsp paprika
salt and freshly ground black pepper
8 quail, oven-ready
small bunch fresh sage
12 rashers of streaky bacon
1 tbsp plain flour
125ml/4fl oz/½ cup red wine
250ml/9fl oz/1 cup chicken stock
1 tsp soft brown sugar

Whisk together the oil, lemon juice and paprika in a small bowl and season well with salt and pepper. Pour over the quail, rubbing it inside and out, then leave to marinate in the fridge for 30 minutes.

Preheat the oven to 190°C/375°F/Gas 5. Put the quail in a roasting tin. Place 2-3 sage leaves on each bird, reserving some to garnish. Lay rashers of bacon on top and roast for 25 minutes in the oven. To test if the birds are cooked, pierce the thickest part of the thigh with a knife or skewer. The juices should run clear; if not, roast for another 5 minutes, then retest. Transfer to a serving plate and keep warm. Fry the reserved sage leaves in a little oil until crisp and set aside.

To make the gravy, place the roasting tin over a low heat, stir in the flour and cook for 1 minute. Gradually stir in the wine and stock and cook, stirring, until the mixture thickens, then stir in the sugar and season with salt and pepper to taste. Pour into a jug and serve with the quail, garnished with the fried sage leaves.

# Rabbit stewed with tomatoes and garlic

**SERVES 4**
2-3 tbsp olive oil
675g/1½lb rabbit, jointed
175g/6oz baby onions, peeled
3 cloves garlic, sliced
400g/14oz can chopped tomatoes,
175ml/6fl oz/¾ cup red wine
2 bay leaves
2-3 sprigs of fresh thyme
2 tsp paprika
salt and freshly ground black pepper

Heat 2 tbsp of the oil in a large pan or flameproof casserole dish. Add the pieces of rabbit and fry over a medium heat until browned all over. Remove from the pan and set aside.

Reduce the heat, add the remaining oil if necessary, then add the onions and fry gently for 4-5 minutes until well browned. Add the garlic and fry for a further 2 minutes, then add the tomatoes, red wine, bay leaves, sprigs of thyme and paprika. Season well with salt and and pepper.

Return the rabbit to the pan, bring to the boil, then lower the heat, cover and simmer gently for about 1 hour, until the rabbit is tender. Check the seasoning and serve.

# Winter

Winter is the time to stay in and enjoy warming substantial meals. The wonderful roots and tubers that now fill greengrocers' shelves make a hearty foundation for such feasts. The colder months are one of the best times to indulge in that tastiest and most versatile of tubers, the potato - boiled, mashed or roasted. Parsnips, celeriac, salsifies and Jerusalem artichokes, each with their own distinctive flavour, are wonderful too for providing substance and comfort, either on their own or mixed together. The other family of vegetables to take full advantage of in winter is the brassicas. These include green, white and red cabbages, Asian greens, kale, Swiss chard, Brussels sprouts and cauliflowers. Chicory and radicchio lend a juicy freshness to winter salads, while tender sweet leeks add an uplifting tang to numerous savoury dishes, as well as making a satisfying accompaniment to rich meaty dishes. Also now at hand are bright-red cranberries and earthy chestnuts, for creating some of the most delicious desserts.

# cabbages

Properly cooked, cabbages are one of the joys of winter. Although available for most of the year, with different varieties arriving in different seasons, it is in the cold winter months that cabbages really come into their own. Winter is also a time when one of the most glorious of all cabbages comes into season – dark-green crinkly-leafed savoy.

Part of the brassica family, along with kale, broccoli and Brussels sprouts, cabbages come in many shapes and forms, from the tightly packed, round heads of white cabbages to sweet pointed cabbages and dark purplish-red specimens with creamy-veined leaves.

Sometimes hearty and robust, sometimes sweet and delicate, cabbages make a good partner for roasted meats and warming stews and sit perfectly alongside roasted, boiled or mashed root vegetables. It is a very versatile ingredient. Delicious served as an accompaniment, it also works well in soups, such as the Italian *ribollita* and Asian stir-fries. It can even be pickled and served as a relish, such as in German *sauerkraut* and Korean *kimchi*. Leftovers are often fried with cold potatoes to make the classic bubble and squeak or can be combined with mashed potatoes and sautéed onions, then shaped into a patty and fried to make the Irish dish colcannon.

## Stuffed cabbage leaves (opposite)

**SERVES 4**

1 savoy or other green cabbage
400g/14oz good-quality pork sausages
3 shallots, finely chopped
25g/1oz breadcrumbs
pinch of freshly grated nutmeg
2 tbsp grated Parmesan cheese
salt and freshly ground black pepper
pinch of dried thyme, or the leaves from a few sprigs of fresh thyme
400g/14oz can chopped tomatoes
80ml/2½fl oz/⅓ cup white wine

Cut away the core from the cabbage and carefully peel away the leaves, keeping them whole. Blanch the leaves by plunging them into boiling water for about 2 minutes, until just tender. Drain well and set aside.

Squeeze the sausage meat from the skins and combine with the shallots, breadcrumbs, nutmeg and Parmesan cheese in a bowl. Season with black pepper, then shape the mixture into eight egg-shaped balls.

Wrap each ball in 1 or 2 cabbage leaves and arrange in the bottom of a large pan or flameproof casserole dish. Sprinkle over the thyme, then pour over the tomatoes and wine and season with salt and pepper to taste. Cover and simmer for about 1 hour. Serve hot.

# Thai-style duck curry with cabbage

**SERVES 4**

1.2 litres/2¼ pints/4¾ cups chicken stock
1 tbsp sweet chilli sauce
3 kaffir lime leaves, shredded
2 red chillies, seeded and finely chopped
1 lemongrass stalk, finely chopped
1 shallot, finely chopped
1 clove garlic, finely chopped
2 duck breasts, about 200g/7oz each
salt
2 tbsp Thai fish sauce
1 tsp soft brown sugar
juice of ½-1 lime
150g/5½oz savoy or pointed cabbage, shredded
3 carrots, sliced diagonally
225g/8oz cauliflower or broccoli, cut into bite-size florets
rice, to serve

Put the chicken stock, chilli sauce, lime leaves, chillies, lemongrass, shallot and garlic in a pan, bring to the boil, then reduce the heat and leave to simmer for about 20 minutes.

Meanwhile, score the skin of the duck breasts and rub with salt. Heat a large frying pan and add the duck, skin-side down. Cook for 10 minutes, then turn over and cook for a further 3-4 minutes. Remove to a board, leave to cool slightly and cut into bite-size pieces.

Drain the stock into a clean pan, then stir in the fish sauce, sugar and lime juice to taste. Add the shredded cabbage, carrots, cauliflower or broccoli florets and the chopped duck. Cover and simmer for about 3 minutes, until the vegetables are tender but still crisp. Serve immediately with rice.

## coleslaw

A classic crunchy coleslaw makes a perfect, refreshing winter salad. To prepare, shred ½ white cabbage and combine with 3 grated carrots, 1 thinly sliced red onion and a handful of sultanas. In a separate bowl, combine 10 tablespoons of mayonnaise with the grated rind and juice of ½ lemon. Stir this mixture into the vegetables to combine well, chill and serve.

**NOTES**

## cabbage braised with wine and pancetta

This is one of the simplest and most delicious methods of cooking cabbages, and savoy or pointed cabbages are particularly good served in this way. Sprouts and kale may be given the same treatment too. For a vegetarian version, shredded sun-dried tomatoes can be substituted for the pancetta. Simply fry a few handfuls of chopped pancetta in 2 tablespoons of olive oil for 2 minutes, then add 3 finely chopped shallots and cook for a further 3-4 minutes. Shred a medium-sized cabbage and toss into the pan, then cook, stirring, for about 3 minutes. Pour over a large glass of white wine, season with salt and pepper to taste, cover and cook for about 10 minutes until the cabbage is sweet, juicy and tender, but not soft. Serve immediately.

# Sweet-and-sour red cabbage

**Red cabbage cooked with apple is a delicious vibrant accompaniment to roast meats. The rich lively flavours make it particularly well suited to fattier meats such as goose, duck and pork, although it is also great with leaner poultry such as chicken and turkey and it is wonderful served cold with wafer-thin slices of cooked ham. Unlike most green and white cabbages, which generally suit fairly brief cooking, red cabbages are quite tough, so should be stewed slowly and gently for a long period of time.**

**SERVES 4**

2 tbsp olive oil
1 onion, chopped
2 cloves garlic, finely chopped
1 cooking apple, peeled and diced
⅓ large red cabbage, thinly sliced
250ml/9fl oz/1 cup red wine
½ tbsp soft brown sugar
2 tbsp red-wine vinegar
2 whole cloves
5 juniper berries, crushed
2-3 tbsp sultanas
salt and freshly ground black pepper

Heat the oil in a large pan. Add the onion and garlic and cook gently for about 5 minutes until soft. Toss in the apple, cabbage, wine, sugar, vinegar, cloves, juniper berries and sultanas. Season to taste with salt and pepper and stir to combine.

Bring to a gentle simmer, cover and leave to cook for about 40-45 minutes, stirring once or twice during the cooking time, until the cabbage is really tender and sweet. If necessary, add a splash more water towards the end of the cooking time to prevent the cabbage sticking to the base of the pan. Check the seasoning, add extra salt and pepper if needed and serve hot or cold.

# kale

Another member of the cabbage family, hardy kale thrives in the depths of winter when little
else will grow, and is available from late autumn right through until early spring. Its flavour, in
fact, improves after a good frost, making it perfect as a cold-weather treat. There are several
varieties, including the widely available dark-green curly kale with its sprawling stems and the
less common blue-green "black" kale, better known as *cavalo nero*. Like cabbage, it is good
served as an accompaniment, but is also delicious added to soups, such as the classic Italian
*ribollita*, and the similar Portuguese *caldo verde*.

To prepare kale, strip out the tough, stringy central stalks and keep only the dark-green
leaves. Shred coarsely and cook in boiling salted water for about 4 minutes, until just tender.
Drain well, then melt some butter in a pan, toss in the cooked kale and cook for another
1–2 minutes to heat through. Season with plenty of black pepper and serve immediately.

## Portuguese kale soup (opposite)

**Based on the classic Portuguese soup *caldo verde*, this hearty soup is a fabulous way
to use up the green curly kale that proliferates on greengrocers' shelves during the cold
winter months. Other cabbages, such as savoy or *cavalo nero*, will do just as well in this
recipe, so substitute it if available. Or, if an Italian-style *ribollita* is preferred, just add a
can of chopped tomatoes with the stock, and use a can of drained cannellini beans in
place of the potatoes. Blend half the beans to thicken the soup, and leave the rest whole.**

**SERVES 4**
600g/1lb 5oz floury potatoes
2 tbsp olive oil
4 cloves garlic, finely chopped
1 onion, finely chopped
1.2 litres/2¼ pints/4¾ cups
vegetable stock
225g/8oz kale, shredded
salt and freshly ground black pepper
8 thin slices chorizo, cut
into strips

Peel and chop the potatoes, then set on one side. Heat the oil
in a large pan. Add the garlic and onion and gently fry for about
5 minutes, until soft. Add the potatoes and stock and leave to
simmer gently for about 20 minutes, until the potatoes are tender.

Transfer to a food processor or blender and process until
smooth. Return to the pan. Stir in the kale and cook for about
10 minutes until the kale is tender, but not soft. Season to taste
with salt and pepper, then ladle the soup into warm serving
bowls, Scatter over the chorizo and serve.

*Winter*

**NOTES**

# brussels sprouts

Growing up a thick central stalk, Brussels sprouts are in fact tiny cabbages with tightly packed leaves. They help brighten up the chilly months, providing an elegant alternative to their larger relations, and are a traditional favourite on the winter festive table. Like all members of the cabbage family, they can reveal sulphurous undertones if overcooked but, when cooked to perfection, they are truly sweet and tender. The green leaves shooting from the top of the stalks – known as sprout tops – can also be eaten, traditionally at the end of winter when all the sprouts themselves have been picked off.

When buying, look for small, firm specimens with fresh-looking leaves and avoid any that are yellowing. To prepare, remove the sprouts from the stalks and peel away any tough outer leaves to reveal the crisp, tightly packed heads. Some people cut a cross into the base to help heat to penetrate and speed up cooking, but this is really unnecessary. To cook whole, boil in salted water for about 5 minutes until just tender, then toss with butter and toasted flaked almonds or hazelnuts, if liked. Bear in mind that sprouts will continue to cook in their residual heat after draining, so be careful not to overdo them. As well as boiled, sprouts can be stir-fried, cooked then mixed into a creamy sauce for a gratin, or made into soup. Sprout tops are best lightly steamed and served tossed in a little butter with a sprinkling of black pepper.

## Fragrant stir-fried sprouts

**SERVES 4**

2 tbsp vegetable oil
2 rashers of streaky bacon, snipped into small pieces
2 cloves garlic, sliced
1 tsp coriander seeds, lightly crushed
450g/1lb Brussels sprouts, shredded
salt and freshly ground black pepper

Heat the oil in a wok, then add the bacon pieces and fry for about 2 minutes until golden. Toss in the garlic and coriander seeds and toss over the heat for a further 30 seconds or so.

Add the shredded sprouts and stir-fry for 1-2 minutes, until they are just tender. Season to taste with salt and pepper and serve immediately.

NOTES

# cauliflowers

Available almost all year round, with different varieties arriving in each season, the creamy-white cauliflower with its encircling band of thick green leaves is another member of the cabbage family that is a staple of the colder months. Like broccoli, the tightly packed cauliflower head consists of unopened flower buds.

Delicious eaten raw or lightly cooked in salads, or served as crudités and used to scoop up creamy dips, cauliflowers are amazingly versatile. Originating in Arabia, they suit both European-style cooking and the spices of the East. In Indonesia, they are blanched, added to the classic salad *gado gado* and served with spicy peanut dressing. In the Middle East, they may be pickled with salt, vinegar and chillies or deep-fried as fritters. The cooked florets are often paired with a creamy or cheesy sauce or may be sprinkled with chopped hard-boiled eggs or garlicky breadcrumbs.

Winter varieties of cauliflowers usually have a more pronounced flavour than those grown in other seasons. When buying, look out for crisp young heads, surrounded by fresh-looking green leaves, and avoid those with dark spots. To prepare, trim away the tough outer leaves and leave small heads whole or break larger ones into florets. Either steam or blanch in boiling salted water for a few minutes until sweet and tender, but still retaining some bite. Be careful not to overcook.

### cauliflower cheese

To make a simple cheesy cauliflower gratin, just cut a large head of a cauliflower into florets and boil in salted water for about 5 minutes until tender. Then drain well and toss with about 4 tablespoons of crème fraîche and about 55g/2oz of grated Gruyère cheese. Season to taste with salt and freshly ground black pepper and turn into an ovenproof dish. Sprinkle over another 55g/2oz of grated Gruyère, grind over a little more black pepper and bake in a preheated oven at 200°C/400°F/Gas 6 for about 15 minutes until golden and bubbling.

**NOTES**

# Piccalilli

**There are numerous cauliflower pickles, from Middle Eastern *torshi*, a spicy ruby-stained mix of cabbages and cauliflowers coloured with beetroot, to this bright-yellow sweet and fragrant piccalilli packed with crispy diced vegetables.**

**MAKES ABOUT 1.8KG/4LB**
225g/8oz salt
1 cauliflower, cut into small florets
350g/12oz silverskin onions, peeled
115g/4oz gherkins, diced
900g/2lb mixed vegetables, such as cucumbers, green beans, courgettes, green peppers and celeriac, prepared and diced
750ml/26fl oz/3 cups cider vinegar
150g/5½oz sugar
2 tsp mustard powder
1 tsp coriander seeds, crushed
1 tsp ground ginger
2 cloves garlic, finely chopped
25g/1oz plain flour
½ tbsp ground turmeric

Put the salt and 2.5 litres/4 pints/10 cups water in a large bowl and stir until the salt has dissolved. Add the cauliflower, onions, gherkins and mixed vegetables, stir, then weight down with a plate and leave to soak for 24 hours. Drain, rinse thoroughly in cold water and drain again.

Put the vinegar, sugar, mustard powder, coriander seeds, ginger and garlic in a large pan and heat gently, stirring, until the sugar has dissolved. Add the drained vegetables, bring to the boil, then reduce the heat and simmer gently for about 7 minutes.

Mix the flour and turmeric with about 4 tablespoons cold water in a small bowl, then stir this mixture into the pan of vegetables and leave to simmer for another 5 minutes, until thick.

Spoon the mixture into warmed sterilized jars, cover, seal and label. Store in a cool dark place for at least 2 weeks before serving. Once a jar is opened, store in the refrigerator.

## cauliflower pakoras

In India, cauliflower florets, coated in a spiced batter and deep-fried, make a popular snack. To prepare, put 150g/5½oz of chickpea flour in a bowl with 25g/1oz of self-raising flour, 2 teaspoons of ground cumin and a pinch of ground turmeric and stir to combine. Gradually whisk in 350ml/12fl oz/1½ cups of cold water to make a smooth batter. Dip the cauliflower florets in the batter and deep-fry in hot oil for about 5 minutes until puffed up and golden. Serve with mango chutney or *raita*.

# leeks

Long creamy leeks with their mild oniony flavour make their first appearance in the closing days of autumn and last through winter into the spring. They may be sold still muddy from the earth with their green outer leaves still attached, or washed and neatly trimmed, and they range in size from tiny delicate sticks, about the size of a large spring onion, to long fat giants. Chopped, they can be used like onions to add a refreshing tang to any dish, such as an omelette, savoury tart, gratin or soup. Cooked whole, then wrapped in ham and baked in a creamy sauce, they are transformed into a superb supper dish. But they are also delicious served on their own as a vegetable accompaniment, sautéed or even braised in a splash of wine.

Most recipes call only for the pale, tightly furled part of the leek, while the tough, green outer leaves are usually discarded. Even leeks sold cleaned up are likely to have some soil still trapped between their closely wrapped layers, so always wash them well before using. Slit down the top of the leek lengthways, then wash under cold running water, flushing out all traces of dirt. If a recipe calls for sliced leeks, cut them up first, then rinse away any soil.

## Leek and sun-dried tomato frittata (opposite)

**SERVES 4**
2 tbsp olive oil
3 leeks, thinly sliced
6 sun-dried (sun-blushed) tomatoes in olive oil, drained and shredded
handful of fresh flat-leaf parsley, roughly chopped, plus extra to garnish
salt and freshly ground black pepper
6 eggs, beaten

Heat the olive oil in a 22.5cm/9in-diameter frying pan. Add the leeks and cook gently for about 10 minutes until tender. Stir in the sun-dried tomatoes and parsley and season well with salt and pepper.

Preheat the grill to hot. Pour the eggs over the vegetables in the frying pan, stirring slightly to combine. Cook gently for about 10 minutes, pulling the edges in as they set and allowing the uncooked egg to run underneath, until the bottom is firm but the frittata is still moist on top.

Place the frittata under the grill and cook for about 5 minutes until set and golden on top. Carefully turn out of the pan on to a plate, then flip over on to another plate so it sits right-side up. Garnish with parsley, cut into wedges and serve.

**NOTES**

# Glamorgan sausages

**SERVES 4**

2 tbsp sunflower oil, plus extra for
frying
2 leeks, finely chopped
150g/5½oz breadcrumbs, plus extra
for coating
150g/5½oz Caerphilly cheese,
crumbled
½ tsp dried oregano
salt and freshly ground black pepper
2 eggs, beaten

**FOR THE SAUCE**

2 tbsp olive oil
½ onion, finely chopped
400g/14oz can chopped tomatoes
3 tbsp vermouth
pinch of sugar
½ tsp dried oregano

Heat 1 tablespoon of the oil in a pan. Add the leeks and cook gently for about 7 minutes, until tender. Tip into a bowl and combine with the breadcrumbs, cheese and oregano, seasoning to taste with salt and pepper. Gradually add some of the beaten eggs, until the mixture comes together but is not too wet.

Shape the mixture into 8 sausages, then dip them in the remaining beaten egg and roll in breadcrumbs to coat. Leave in the fridge to chill for at least 30 minutes.

Meanwhile make the sauce. Heat the oil in a pan, add the onion and fry for about 5 minutes, until soft. Toss in the tomatoes, vermouth, sugar and oregano, then season to taste with salt and pepper and leave to simmer gently for about 20 minutes. Set aside and keep warm.

Heat a little sunflower oil in a large frying pan. Add the chilled sausages and cook for about 5-7 minutes, until crisp and golden all over. Serve immediately with the sauce.

# Vichyssoise

**Leeks seem to have been created for turning into soups - and there are countless recipes. This French classic is traditionally served chilled, but can be heated up on colder days.**

**SERVES 4**

55g/2oz butter
1 onion, chopped
3 large leeks, sliced
1 potato, cut into chunks
750ml/26fl oz/3 cups vegetable
stock
300ml/10½fl oz/1¼ cups milk
8-10 tbsp single cream
juice of ½ lemon
salt and freshly ground black pepper
small handful of fresh chives,
chopped, to garnish

Melt the butter in a large pan. Add the onion and leeks, then fry gently for about 5 minutes, until tender. Add the potato and stock, cover and leave to simmer for about 15 minutes, until the potato is tender.

Tip the contents of the pan into a blender or food processor and process until smooth. Transfer to a large bowl, stir in the milk, cream and lemon juice and season to taste with salt and pepper. Leave to chill in the fridge for at least 2 hours.

The soup will have thickened on standing, so add a splash more milk if needed. Check the seasoning and add extra salt, pepper and lemon juice if needed. Serve sprinkled with the chives.

**NOTES**

# Trout baked in paper with leeks and carrots

**SERVES 4**
2 tbsp sunflower oil
2 large leeks, finely sliced
2.5cm/1in piece fresh ginger, peeled
and finely grated
3 carrots, cut into fine matchsticks
1 tsp sesame oil
salt and freshly ground black pepper
4 trout fillets, about 175g/6oz each,
skinned
juice of 1½ limes

Preheat the oven to 200°C/400°F/Gas 6 and cut out four 35cm/14in squares of greaseproof paper.

Heat the oil in a pan, add the leeks and ginger and fry gently for about 10 minutes, until soft. Stir in the carrots and sesame oil, season to taste with salt and pepper and remove from the heat. Divide the vegetables among the sheets of greaseproof paper, making a pile in the centre of each sheet.

Lay a fillet of fish on top of each pile of vegetables, season with salt and pepper and sprinkle with lime juice. Fold the paper over the fish, twisting the edges together to make a tightly sealed parcel. Place on a baking sheet and bake in the oven for about 15 minutes, until the fish is cooked through. Put each parcel on to a warm plate and serve immediately.

# Cock-a-leekie

**This traditional Scottish soup, which comes somewhere between a chunky broth and a wholesome stew, makes the most of some of winter's finest ingredients, combining barley, chicken, tender leeks and sweet juicy prunes.**

**SERVES 4**
100g/3½oz pearl barley
1.2 litres/2¼ pints/4¾ cups
chicken stock
1 bay leaf
1 tsp dried thyme
4 juniper berries, crushed
3 large leeks, sliced
100g/3½oz ready-to-eat prunes, cut
into bite-size pieces
400g/14oz cooked chicken, cut into
bite-size pieces
freshly ground black pepper

Put the barley, stock, bay leaf, thyme and juniper berries in a large pan, bring to the boil, then reduce the heat, cover and leave to simmer for about 25 minutes, until the barley is tender.

Add the leeks, prunes and chicken, recover and allow to simmer for about 10 minutes, until the leeks are tender. Season with plenty of black pepper, ladle into bowls and serve.

# swiss chard

A member of the beetroot family, lush leafy Swiss chard is available from late autumn through into spring. With its thick, juicy, white stems and dark-green leaves, it offers a lighter alternative to other winter greens. You can also find red chard, with pinky-red stalks and veins, but despite its stunning appearance, its flavour is less good than that of the white-stalked green variety.

Chard leaves have a similar taste to spinach, although are more robust in texture, and the juicy stalks are tender and mild, not unlike asparagus. Look for mature leaves with thick, lush stems. Smaller specimens with thinner stalks are good too, but the juicy stems are one of the main delights of chard. Leaves should be shiny; avoid any with dark or slimy spots.

Cut off the tough tips of the stems, wash thoroughly and drain well, shaking off as much water as possible, before cooking. Young tender chard leaves can be cooked whole, but with older ones the tougher stem should be cut off, sliced and tossed into the pan for a minute or so before the softer green part of the leaf. Chard, like spinach, reduces significantly with cooking, so allow what may seem to be an over-generous quantity per person.

## Swiss chard with tomatoes, chickpeas and spicy sausage

**SERVES 4**

600g/1lb 5oz spicy pork sausages
2 tbsp olive oil
1 onion, chopped
3 cloves garlic, chopped
400g/14oz can chopped tomatoes
400g/14oz can chickpeas, drained and rinsed
500g/1lb 2oz Swiss chard, sliced
crusty bread, to serve

Heat the grill until hot and use to cook the sausages for about 10-15 minutes until well browned all over. Slice into 1cm/½in-thick chunks and set aside.

Heat the oil in a large pan. Add the onion and garlic and fry gently for about 5 minutes, until soft. Add the tomatoes, chickpeas and sausages and leave to simmer for about 10 minutes. Toss in the Swiss chard and cook for a further 10 minutes, stirring occasionally, until the leaves are tender. Serve piping hot with crusty bread.

NOTES

# chicory (belgian endive) and radicchio

These two crisp salad vegetables are related and, despite their differences in appearance, share a distinctive bitter flavour. Because chicory is often referred to by its French name, *endive*, it is often confused with curly endive, or *frisée*, which consists of loosely packed, crisp, curly, green fronds and is mainly used as a salad leaf. Plump, bullet-shaped Belgian endive, or chicory, with its tightly packed, green- or yellow-tinged white leaves, is used in both salads and cooked dishes. Chicory was originally grown just for its bitter roots, which were ground and added to coffee. Belgian endive is the shoot of the plant, first cultivated in Belgium and grown in darkness to achieve its pale colour and more mellow flavour.

Vibrant red radicchio, with its white-veined leaves, may also be used in salads or cooked, although it has a more bitter flavour than chicory.

Although chicory and radicchio, are available all year, they are particularly valuable in the winter, when so few other fresh salad leaves are available. The long pointed leaves of chicory are also excellent served as part of a selection of crudités for scooping up creamy dips. The whole heads are excellent cooked too, either braised, roasted or baked in a gratin.

Choose only firm white chicory, avoiding any that is beginning to wilt or turn brown. Radicchio should be a rich red, also without any brown patches. To prepare, slice off the root end, rinse and pat dry with kitchen paper, then use according to the recipe or divide into leaves for a salad.

### roast buttered chicory

Allow 1 large or 2 small heads of chicory per person. Cut large heads into quarters and small ones in half, then arrange in a baking dish and cover with thin shavings of butter. Season well with salt and pepper, cover, then bake in a preheated oven at 190°C/375°F/Gas 5 until tender and golden. This simple method of preparation can also be used to turn radicchio into something extra-special.

NOTES

# Chicory salad with pear and walnut

It is easy to miss the refreshing taste of crunchy salads and sweet juicy fruits during the colder months of the year, so this crisp zesty salad provides a really special treat. Served as an appetizer or accompaniment, it offers a delicious contrast to winter's hearty root vegetables, brassicas and stews.

**SERVES 4**
4 small handfuls of watercress
4 heads of chicory (Belgian endive)
2 pears
55g/2oz walnut pieces
25g/1oz Parmesan or Pecorino cheese, shaved

**FOR THE DRESSING**
1½ tbsp lemon juice
½ tsp honey
4 tbsp olive oil
salt and freshly ground black pepper

First make the dressing by whisking together the lemon juice, honey and olive oil in small bowl. Season to taste with salt and pepper and set aside.

Put a handful of watercress on each serving plate. Divide the chicory into leaves and arrange on top. Peel and core the pears, then slice into slim wedges and scatter these over the leaves.

Scatter the walnuts and cheese shavings on top, then drizzle over the dressing and serve.

# Creamy baked chicory

You can use either chicory or radicchio in this recipe. Baked with crème fraîche and Parmesan cheese, either vegetable makes a great partner to robust meat and game dishes.

**SERVES 4**
4 large heads of chicory (Belgian endive) or radicchio
125ml/4fl oz/½ cup crème fraîche
55g/2oz Parmesan cheese, grated
freshly ground black pepper

Preheat the oven to 200°C/400°F/Gas 6. Halve the chicory or radicchio heads lengthways and plunge into a pan of boiling salted water for about 2 minutes. Drain well and pat dry with kitchen paper.

Arrange in a baking dish, spoon the crème fraîche over the top, sprinkle with the Parmesan and pepper to taste, then bake in the oven for about 15 minutes, until the chicory or radicchio is tender and the dish is crisp and well browned on top. Serve.

# asian greens

A whole array of Asian greens is widely available right through the winter months. They are fabulous cooked lightly in Asian-style broths and stir-fries, or simple served on their own as a vegetable accompaniment. Many are related to the cabbage family.

*Pak choi*, *choi sum* and Chinese broccoli all have dark-green leaves and a mild flavour and are good stir-fried, added to soups or blanched as well as served alone, perhaps drizzled with a little sesame oil and a sprinkling of chilli. Chinese mustard greens have a more fiery flavour, with a distinct mustardy punch. Young leaves may be added to salads, while older leaves are better stir-fried. Pale-green Chinese leaves grow in large heads, rather like an elongated lettuce with a thick central rib. The leaves are tender, while the white rib is crisp. The vegetable has a faintly cabbage-like flavour and is good sliced and added to salads or stir-fried for a few minutes until just tender but retaining some bite.

When choosing any Asian greens, look for fresh-looking specimens with lush green leaves. Avoid any that are wilting, yellowing or have soft slimy patches. Depending on size, *pak choi* can be cooked whole, halved, divided into separate leaves or sliced. Its thick stems require slightly longer cooking than the dark-green leaves, so these are usually added to the pan a few minutes before the rest. *Choi sum* should be trimmed of its stalks and the leaves shredded before cooking. Chinese broccoli can be divided into florets, stems and leaves (which should be shredded), all of which can be cooked separately. To prepare Chinese leaves, simply slice as thickly as required across the head.

## pak choi with coconut dressing

This delicious vegetable accompaniment is very quick to prepare. Just combine 4 tablespoons of coconut milk with the juice of ½ lime and 1 teaspoon of Oriental fish sauce. If liked, add ½ chopped, seeded red chilli as well. Divide the *pak choi* into leaves, then plunge into boiling water for 30–60 seconds until the leaves are just starting to wilt. Drain well, then drizzle with the coconut dressing. Toss to combine and serve immediately.

NOTES

# Stir-fried pak choi with garlic and gingered beef

**Also known as *bok choy*, horse's ear and Chinese celery cabbage, *pak choi* is probably one of the most widely available Asian greens. You can, however, substitute others in this recipe. If a more fiery result is preferred, try using Chinese mustard greens, or for a milder, sweeter flavour, use Chinese leaves instead of the *pak choi*.**

**SERVES 4**

2 cloves garlic, crushed
2.5cm/1in piece fresh ginger, peeled and grated
2 red chillies, seeded and finely chopped
1 tbsp Oriental fish sauce
1 tsp sesame oil
1 tbsp soft brown sugar
3 tbsp sunflower oil
450g/1lb fillet steak
4 large heads of *pak choi*
steamed rice or noodles, to serve

Prepare a marinade by combining the garlic, ginger, chillies, fish sauce, sesame oil, sugar and 1 tbsp of the sunflower oil in a small bowl. Set aside.

Place the steak between two sheets of clear film and beat with a mallet or rolling pin until thin. Cut into thin strips. Add to the marinade, toss to combine and leave in the fridge to marinate for at least 1 hour.

Divide the *pak choi* into leaves. Cut off the white fleshy part and slice diagonally. Also slice up the larger leaves. Set aside.

Heat 1 tablespoon of the remaining oil in a wok. Add the beef with the marinade and stir-fry for 2-3 minutes until medium-rare, then remove to a warmed plate. If necessary, add a little more oil to the wok, then add the white part of the *pak choi* and stir-fry for about 1 minute. Add the green part of the leaves and stir-fry for a further 30 seconds, or until the leaves start to wilt. Toss in the beef, check the seasoning, then serve with rice or noodles.

# potatoes

Potatoes have been a staple in Europe since they were imported in the 16th century from South America, where they had been cultivated for several thousand years. Their popularity spread rapidly and, as a result, there are countless classic dishes in which they are the central ingredient, ranging from Irish champ and Scottish stovies to the French *pommes dauphinoises*. They are also delicious simply boiled or steamed and served with a knob of butter and a sprinkling of fresh herbs, or mashed with butter and milk. Par-boiled and roasted in oil, they become wonderfully crisp and golden on the outside, while remaining floury and light inside. Thinly sliced and baked with onions and cream, they make a perfect partner to roasted meats, or try baking them whole, then stuffing them with all manner of savoury fillings. Sometimes they are added to soups and stews as a thickener, and are even used in pudding and cakes.

Always choose firm specimens with few blemishes and store in a cool, dark place until ready to use. The flesh of potatoes discolours when exposed to air, so either peel and prepare just before using, or peel and leave in a large bowl of cold water until ready to cook.

## rösti potatoes

These elegant little potato cakes are a great accompaniment and also make a stunning appetizer when topped with a dollop of soured cream, a slither of smoked salmon and a sprinkling of chopped chives and lemon juice. To prepare, grate 450g/1lb of floury potatoes and ½ onion into a large bowl. Mix to combine, season well with salt and leave for about 20 minutes. Squeeze hard to extract as much liquid as possible, then mix in 1 egg, 2 tablespoons of plain flour and some freshly ground black pepper.

Heat about 2.5cm/1in of oil in a large frying pan. Add several tablespoons of the potato mixture, shaping them into cakes with the back of the spoon, and fry for 1-2 minutes on each side, until crisp and golden. Drain on kitchen paper and keep warm while you cook the remaining mixture in the same way. Serve immediately.

**NOTES**

# Roast beef with garlic potatoes

**SERVES 4-6**

1.25kg/2lb 12oz potatoes, sliced
(about 3mm/⅛in thick)
25g/1oz butter
4 cloves garlic, thinly sliced
2 tsp fresh thyme leaves
salt and freshly ground black
pepper
420ml/14½fl oz/1¾ cups hot
beef stock
900g/2lb topside of beef

Preheat the oven to 190°C/375°F/Gas 5 and grease a large baking dish. Arrange a layer of potatoes in the bottom of the dish, dot with a little butter and scatter over some garlic and thyme. Repeat with layers of potato, butter, garlic and thyme until they are all used up, seasoning as you go with salt and pepper. Pour over the stock. Cover with foil and cook in the oven for about 40 minutes.

Increase the oven temperature to 200°C/400°F/Gas 6 and cook for a further 15 minutes. Meanwhile, season the beef with ground black pepper.

Remove the dish from the oven, uncover and lay the beef on top of the potatoes. Roast for 20 minutes, then reduce the temperature to 190°C/375°F/Gas 5 and cook for a further 20 minutes.

Remove the beef to a board and allow to rest for about 10 minutes before carving, leaving the potatoes in the oven to keep warm while the meat rests. Serve.

# Potato and cauliflower curry

**SERVES 4**

2 tbsp sunflower oil
½ tsp dried chilli flakes
2 cloves garlic, finely chopped
2 tsp grated fresh ginger
450g/1lb potatoes, cut into
1.5-2cm/¾in cubes
125ml/4fl oz/½ cup water
2 tsp ground cumin
1 tsp ground coriander
½ tsp ground turmeric
¼ tsp salt
1 cauliflower, broken into florets
½ lemon
handful of fresh coriander, chopped
rice or Indian breads, to serve

Heat the oil in a pan and fry the chilli flakes for about 10 seconds. Add the garlic and ginger, stir-fry for a further 20 seconds or so and stir in the potatoes.

Pour over the water and stir in the cumin, ground coriander, turmeric and salt. Stir in the cauliflower and bring to the boil. Reduce the heat, cover and simmer gently, stirring occasionally, for about 20 minutes until the vegetables are tender.

Squeeze in lemon juice to taste, sprinkle with fresh coriander and serve with rice or Indian breads.

# celeriac

Knobbly celeriac, with its thick brown skin, may lack visual appeal, but under that outer coating is a mild creamy-white vegetable with a subtle celery-like flavour, that is sweet and crisp when eaten raw and meltingly soft and smooth when cooked. It is delicious made into a purée with butter, cream and seasoning, or roasted with other roots until crisp and golden.

Buy celeriac with the smoothest skin available, so there is less waste when peeling. The skin is thicker than that of other root vegetables and is better peeled off using a sharp knife rather than a vegetable peeler. Cut into quarters first so that the thickness of the skin is clearly visible, then cut it away. Once exposed to air, the creamy flesh discolours rapidly, so put the prepared celeriac straight away into a bowl of water to which a little lemon juice has been added.

## Fish pie topped with creamy celeriac mash (opposite)

**SERVES 4**

2 tbsp olive oil
1 onion, chopped
2 cloves garlic, chopped
2 x 400g/14oz cans chopped tomatoes
½ tsp ground cinnamon
¼ tsp ground turmeric
¼ tsp ground ginger
salt and freshly ground black pepper
300g/10½oz celeriac diced
300g/10½oz carrots, diced
450g/1lb potatoes, diced
25g/1oz butter
2 tbsp crème fraîche
500g/1lb 2oz firm white fish, such as haddock or hoki, skinned
250g/9oz cooked, peeled king prawns

Preheat the oven to 200°C/400°F/Gas 6. Heat the oil in a large pan, add the onion and garlic and fry gently for 5 minutes, until soft. Add the tomatoes, cinnamon, turmeric and ginger and season to taste with salt and pepper. Bring to the boil, then reduce the heat and simmer for about 20 minutes until thick. Set aside.

Meanwhile, put the celeriac, carrots and potatoes in a pan, add 4 tablespoons water, cover tightly and cook, shaking the pan frequently, for about 20 minutes, until the vegetables are tender. Check towards the end of the cooking time and add more water if necessary to prevent the vegetables from burning. Add the butter and mash well, then stir in the crème fraîche and season to taste with salt and pepper.

Put the fish into a clean pan, add enough water just to cover, bring to a gentle simmer and cook for 3-4 minutes, then drain well and flake into large chunks. Gently fold the fish with the prawns into the tomato sauce and transfer to a baking dish.

Spread the celeriac mash over the fish and bake in the oven for about 30 minutes until crisp and golden on top. Serve.

NOTES

# jerusalem artichokes

Unrelated to the globe artichoke (see page 38), the distinctively flavoured Jerusalem artichoke is a knobbly tuber with thin, pale-brown skin and creamy-white flesh. It is a native of North America and was introduced to Europe in the early 17th century.

When cooked, Jerusalem artichokes have a soft, creamy texture, not unlike that of potatoes. With their slightly sweet and nutty flavour, they make a particularly good accompaniment to all kinds of rich meat, poultry and game dishes.

When choosing Jerusalem artichokes, look for firm, smooth, evenly sized specimens. The more knobbly the artichokes, the more waste there will be when peeling them. To prepare, scrub well, then trim off any dark or woody bits and peel thinly. As soon as they have been cut, drop straight into water to which a squeeze of lemon juice has been added. This will prevent the flesh from discolouring when exposed to the air.

Jerusalem artichokes can be boiled like potatoes, then mashed, puréed or made into soup. They are also good tossed in a creamy sauce and baked in a gratin, or roasted in olive oil until crisp and golden. When sliced wafer-thin and deep-fried, they make delicious crunchy crisps for snacking on or scooping up a creamy dip.

## stoved artichokes

In a variation on the classic Scottish dish, stovies, Jerusalem artichokes are delicious steamed with a little fried garlic and stock in a covered pan. Peel about 1kg/2lb 4oz of artichokes, then cut them into chunks. Heat 2 tablespoons of olive oil in a large pan and gently fry a finely chopped clove of garlic for about 1-2 minutes, until soft. Toss in the artichokes, stirring to coat, then add about 2 tablespoons of vegetable stock, a pinch of salt and plenty of freshly ground black pepper. Cover tightly and cook gently for about 10 minutes, stirring occasionally, until tender. Check the seasoning and serve.

NOTES

# Warm Jerusalem artichoke salad

**Piping hot, crisp and golden, Jerusalem artichokes are delicious tossed with fresh salad leaves - giving the substance and warmth needed in a winter salad. Serve this dish as an accompaniment or appetizer, or toss in some extra bacon and a handful of nuts and serve with crusty bread as a light lunch or supper.**

**SERVES 4**
3 tbsp olive oil
800g/1lb 12oz Jerusalem artichokes, cut into chunks
salt and freshly ground black pepper
150g/5½oz salad leaves, such as baby spinach, rocket and watercress
4 rashers of bacon, grilled until crispy

**FOR THE DRESSING**
1 tsp Dijon mustard
1 tsp grated lemon rind
1 tbsp white-wine vinegar
pinch of sugar
3 tbsp olive oil

Preheat the oven to 200°C/400°F/Gas 6. Pour the oil into a roasting tin and place in the oven. Meanwhile, cook the artichokes in boiling salted water for about 10 minutes, until just tender.

Drain the artichokes and allow to steam dry, then tip into the roasting tin. Toss to coat in the oil and cook in the oven for about 25 minutes, tossing from time to time, until crisp and golden.

Meanwhile, make the dressing. Blend together the mustard, lemon rind, vinegar and sugar in a small bowl, then whisk in the olive oil and season to taste with salt and pepper.

Arrange the salad leaves on four serving plates, then scatter over the hot artichokes and snip the bacon over the top. Drizzle with the dressing and serve immediately.

# Spiced Jerusalem artichokes

**SERVES 4**
2 tbsp olive oil
1 onion, halved and thinly sliced
2 cloves garlic, crushed
1 tsp ground cumin
1 tsp ground coriander
large pinch of dried chilli flakes
450g/1lb Jerusalem artichokes, cut into large pieces
salt
60ml/2fl oz/¼ cup water
juice of ¼ lemon

Heat the oil in a large pan. Add the onion and garlic and fry gently for about 5 minutes, until soft. Stir in the ground cumin, ground coriander and chilli flakes and cook for about 30 seconds.

Toss in the Jerusalem artichokes, season to taste with salt and pour over the water. Stir to combine well, bring to a gentle simmer, cover the pan and cook over a low heat for about 20 minutes until the artichokes are tender.

Check the seasoning and add more salt if necessary, then squeeze over the lemon juice and serve.

# parsnips and other roots

The cold winter months are the time really to make the most of root vegetables, which, thankfully, are in plentiful supply then and can be enjoyed in a wealth of hearty warming dishes. Parsnips, turnips, swedes, salsifies and even kohlrabi grace the greengrocers' shelves alongside staples such as potatoes and carrots. They all have their own delicious and distinctive flavour and texture and can be cooked together or separately.

Turnips and swedes are similarly robust vegetables and can often be substituted for each other in recipes. They are both wonderful diced in chunky soups and stews, as well as mashed or roasted. Parsnips have an almost honeyed flavour and go particularly well with warm spices. When they are roasted, their natural sugars caramelize, giving a wonderfully crisp, golden and sticky result.

When choosing root vegetables, look for firm specimens. Buy them still covered in earth if possible, as their flavour will be far better. Avoid any with dark or soft patches. Most roots keep well, but should be stored in a cool dark place to prevent them from sprouting.

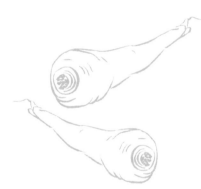

### root vegetable crisps (opposite)

Crisps made from wafer-thin slices of root vegetables are easy to prepare, and are great served with drinks. Serve on their own or with a little dish of garlic mayonnaise for dipping. You can use any root vegetable you like. Try a mix of parsnips and potatoes, for example. Or, for a contrasting dash of colour, add a few carrots and perhaps some beetroot. First prepare the vegetables: trim and peel, then use a mandolin or vegetable peeler to slice them into thin shavings. Rinse well, then pat dry on kitchen paper. Fill a pan about one-third full with sunflower oil and heat to 190°C/375°F. Working in batches, deep fry the vegetables for about 1 minute until crisp and golden. Lift out of the oil using a slotted spoon, and drain on a wire rack covered with several layers of kitchen paper. Sprinkle with salt and serve immediately.

# Curried parsnip soup

**SERVES 4**

2 tbsp olive oil
1 onion, chopped
2 cloves garlic, finely chopped
2.5cm/1in piece fresh ginger, peeled and grated
5 large parsnips, diced
¼ tsp dried chilli flakes
1 tsp ground cumin
1 tsp ground coriander
¼ tsp ground turmeric
1.2 litres/2¼ pints/4¾ cups vegetable stock
juice of ½ lemon
natural yoghurt and naan bread, to serve

Heat the oil in a large pan, then add the onion, garlic and ginger and fry gently for about 5 minutes, until the onion is tender.

Stir in the parsnips, chilli, cumin, coriander and turmeric, then pour over the stock and bring to the boil. Reduce the heat, cover and leave to simmer for about 15 minutes, until the parsnips are tender.

Tip into a blender or food processor and process until smooth. Return to the pan and stir in lemon juice to taste. Ladle into bowls, drizzle with yoghurt and serve with wedges of warm naan bread.

# Sautéed salsify in butter with herbs

**Serve these crisp golden roots as a side dish, or scatter them over a simple salad of winter leaves tossed with grilled spring onions, crispy bacon and a drizzle of vinaigrette.**

**SERVES 4**

600g/1lb 5oz salsifies
salt and freshly ground black pepper
25g/1oz butter
grated rind of 1 lemon
large handful of fresh flat-leaf parsley, roughly chopped

Peel the salsifies and cut into thick 5cm/2in-long batons, placing them in water mixed with a splash of lemon juice to prevent them discolouring, as you go. Bring a pan of salted water to the boil, add the salsify and cook for about 15 minutes until tender, then drain well and leave to steam dry.

In a frying pan, melt the butter until sizzling, then add the cooked roots and sauté for about 5 minutes until crisp and golden. Sprinkle over the lemon rind and parsley, season to taste with black pepper and serve immediately.

**NOTES**

# Salsify mash

**This light and tangy version of classic mash is delicious served with meat and game. The olive oil and lemon juice balance the subtle flavour of the salsifies perfectly.**

**SERVES 4**
600g/1lb 5oz salsifies
2 tbsp olive oil
juice of ½ lemon
salt and freshly ground black pepper

Peel the salsifies and cut into chunks, placing them in water to which a splash of lemon juice has been added to stop them discolouring, as you go. Bring a pan of lightly salted water to the boil. Toss in the salsify chunks and cook for about 15 minutes until tender, then drain well.

Mash the salsifies until smooth, stir in the olive oil and lemon juice to taste and season well with black pepper. Serve.

# Kohlrabi stewed with tomatoes and spices

**Kohlrabi makes a wonderfully rich and hearty stew. During cooking it becomes deliciously sweet and tender, blending well with the juicy tomatoes, flavoursome garlic and warm spices.**

**SERVES 4**
2 tbsp olive oil
2 cloves garlic, finely chopped
1 tsp ground cumin
¼ tsp dried chilli flakes
5 kohlrabi, quartered
400g/14oz can chopped tomatoes
½ tsp ground turmeric
salt and freshly ground black pepper

Heat the oil in a large pan. Add the garlic and fry gently for about 2 minutes, then stir in the cumin and chilli flakes and fry for another 30 seconds.

Stir in the kohlrabi, followed by the tomatoes and turmeric. Season to taste with salt and pepper and bring to the boil. Reduce the heat, cover and leave to simmer for about 30 minutes until the kohlrabi is tender. Serve.

# cranberries

Related to bilberries and blueberries, bright-red oval cranberries are harder and bigger and have a much sharper flavour. They come into season in late autumn and last right through the winter. Always cooked, they are often made into a piquant sauce that is traditionally served with turkey at Christmas and Thanksgiving in the US. The berries are also good for turning into preserves and can be added to innumerable desserts. Because their flavour is naturally sharp, they are often best combined with other fruits. They make, for example, a good addition to apple crumble or pie and are great in cakes and muffins or added to sweetened tea-breads. Their natural astringency adds interest to all these dishes, offsetting the sweetness of other ingredients.

The hard, waxy berries contain a natural preservative, benzoic acid, which means they keep better than most berries. When buying, look for firm, shiny berries, avoiding any that are soft or shrivelled. If adding sugar to cranberries in a recipe, such as a sauce, do so after the berries have cooked a little and "popped", otherwise they will not soften.

## Cranberry and apple muffins (opposite)

**MAKES 12**
375g/13oz self-raising flour
115g/4oz caster sugar
1 tsp ground cinnamon
125ml/4fl oz/½ cup milk
2 large eggs, beaten
115g/4oz butter, melted
1 eating apple, peeled, cored and finely chopped
large handful of fresh cranberries

Preheat the oven to 200ºC/400ºF/Gas 6. Line a 12-hole muffin tin with paper cases.

Sift the flour, caster sugar and cinnamon into a large bowl and make a well in the centre. In a jug, combine the milk, beaten eggs, melted butter and chopped apple. Pour into the well in the flour mixture and mix briefly until just combined.

Drop a spoonful of the mixture into the bottom of each muffin case, top each with a few cranberries, then spoon the remaining mixture on top and sprinkle on a few more cranberries.

Bake in the oven for about 25 minutes until risen and golden. Remove the muffins from the tin and leave on a wire rack to cool slightly before serving.

**NOTES**

# chestnuts

Chestnuts are traditionally given a special place at the Christmas table. These shiny brown nuts are delicious boiled or roasted - always split the hard skin first to stop them exploding while cooking - and eaten on their own. They are also good puréed and served as a side dish or mixed into stuffings. Tossed with freshly cooked Brussels sprouts, a knob of butter and freshly ground black pepper, they make one of the best vegetable dishes on the winter menu.

In southern Europe, they have a long culinary history, being used in breads, cakes and sweetmeats and to make a type of flour. Chestnuts have a natural affinity with chocolate and you will find many recipes for rich chocolate desserts, ice creams and cakes that include them.

Most recipes for chestnuts require them to be cooked and peeled, and although this is simple to do, you can buy ready-prepared chestnuts in cans or vacuum packs. These also have the advantage of being available at any time of the year. Canned chestnut purée is available too.

## Chestnut and hazelnut roast

**SERVES 6-8**
100g/3½oz hazelnuts
2 tbsp olive oil
1 onion, finely chopped
2 cloves garlic, finely chopped
225g/8oz mushrooms, finely chopped
salt and freshly ground black pepper
225g/8oz chestnuts, cooked, peeled and finely chopped
85g/3oz white breadcrumbs
pinch of dried thyme
4 tbsp vegetable stock
juice of ½ lemon

Preheat the oven to 200°C/400°F/Gas 6. Grease a 900g/2lb loaf tin and line the base with greaseproof paper.

Put the hazelnuts in a food processor and process briefly to chop finely, but avoid grinding to a smooth powder. Set aside.

Heat the oil in a large pan, add the onion and garlic and gently fry for about 5 minutes, until tender. Add the mushrooms, sprinkle with a little salt and cook gently for about 10 minutes, until the mushrooms are tender and most of the liquid has evaporated. They should be moist, but not wet.

Remove the pan from the heat and stir in the hazelnuts, chestnuts, breadcrumbs, thyme, stock and lemon juice and season with salt and pepper. Press the mixture into the loaf tin and bake in the oven for about 30 minutes, until golden. Leave the roast to stand for about 5 minutes, then very carefully invert on to a board or serving platter, cut into slices and serve.

**NOTES**

# what's in season when

Seasonality is subject to change and is really something of a moveable feast. The chart opposite will give you an indication of when most fruits and vegetables are likely to come into season and be at their best. But in areas with a warmer-than-average climate compared to the rest of the country, many may be ready to harvest a month or so earlier in the year than is stated.

Also, weather conditions may vary from year to year, causing crops to develop earlier or later than expected. Remember too that cooler-than-average temperatures may, in fact, benefit some crops, by giving them the time to grow more slowly and so develop their flavours to their maximum potential. Others, however, will be hampered in their development without long days of constant sunshine to help them to ripen and sweeten and so achieve their full glory.

A large number of fruits and vegetables is available across several seasons - perhaps arriving on the shelves at the end of winter and lasting right through until the early part of the summer - while others are around only for a couple of months or even weeks. Still more, such as apples, pears and many roots, may be available from cold-storage, tasting just as fresh and delicious as they ever were, long after their peak growing season is over.

Because of the delightful flexibility of nature when it comes to growing seasons, this book should be used only as a guide for what to look out for in the shops and supermarkets as the year progresses. By far the best way of always making sure that you obtain seasonal produce at its very best is to get to know your suppliers - ask them what is likely to be available when, what is grown locally and what is at its freshest and highest quality every time you visit them with your shopping basket. Or you could try growing some produce in your own garden or allotment. The taste of ingredients cooked within hours of picking is truly sensational and can open up a whole new world of surprising depths and subtleties of flavour.

| INGREDIENT | SPRING | SUMMER | AUTUMN | WINTER |
|---|---|---|---|---|
| apples | cold store | cold store | in season | cold store |
| apricots | | in season | | |
| artichokes, globe | in season | in season | in season | |
| artichokes, Jerusalem | | | | in season |
| Asian greens | in season | | in season | in season |
| asparagus | in season | | | |
| aubergines | | in season | in season | |
| avocados | in season | in season | in season | in season |
| basil | | in season | | |
| beans | | in season | in season | |
| beetroot | | in season | in season | cold store |
| blackberries | | | in season | |
| blackcurrants | | in season | | |
| blueberries | | in season | | |
| broccoli, calabrese | | in season | in season | |
| broccoli, purple sprouting | in season | in season | | |
| broccoli, romanesco | | in season | in season | |
| Brussels sprouts | | | in season | in season |
| cabbages | in season | in season | in season | in season |
| carrots | in season | in season | in season | cold store |
| cauliflowers | in season | in season | in season | in season |
| celeriac | | | in season | in season |
| celery | | | in season | |
| cherries | | in season | | |
| chestnuts | | | in season | in season |
| chicory | in season | | in season | in season |
| chives | in season | in season | | |
| coriander | in season | in season | | |
| corn | | in season | in season | |
| courgettes | | in season | in season | |
| crab apples | | | in season | |
| cranberries | | | in season | in season |
| cucumbers | | in season | In season | |

| INGREDIENT | SPRING | SUMMER | AUTUMN | WINTER |
|---|---|---|---|---|
| dandelion leaves | in season | in season | | |
| dill | in season | in season | | |
| elderberries | | | in season | |
| elderflowers | | in season | | |
| endive, curly | in season | in season | in season | in season |
| fennel | | | in season | |
| figs | | | in season | |
| game | | | in season | |
| garlic | in season | in season | cold store | cold store |
| garlic, wild | in season | | | |
| gooseberries | | in season | | |
| grapes | | | in season | |
| kale | | | | in season |
| kohlrabi | | in season | in season | in season |
| lamb | in season | in season | in season | in season |
| leeks | in season | | in season | in season |
| lettuces | in season | in season | | |
| marjoram | in season | in season | | |
| medlars | | | in season | |
| melons | | in season | in season | |
| mint | in season | in season | in season | |
| morels | in season | | | |
| mushrooms | | | in season | |
| nettles | in season | | | |
| okra | | in season | | |
| onions | cold store | cold store | in season | cold store |
| oregano | in season | in season | | |
| parsley | in season | in season | in season | |
| parsnips | | | in season | in season |
| peaches | | in season | in season | |
| pears | cold store | | in season | cold store |
| peas | | in season | | |
| peppers | | in season | in season | |

| INGREDIENT | SPRING | SUMMER | AUTUMN | WINTER |
|---|---|---|---|---|
| plums | | | in season | |
| pomegranates | | | in season | |
| potatoes | cold store | cold store | in season | in season |
| potatoes, new | in season | | | |
| pumpkins | | | in season | |
| quinces | | | in season | |
| raspberries | | in season | | |
| redcurrants | | in season | | |
| rhubarb | in season | | | in season |
| rocket | in season | in season | in season | in season |
| rosehips | | | in season | |
| rosemary | | in season | in season | |
| sage | in season | in season | in season | in season |
| salsifies | | | in season | in season |
| shallots | | in season | in season | |
| sloes | | | in season | |
| sorrel | in season | in season | | |
| spinach | in season | in season | in season | in season |
| spring greens | in season | | | |
| spring onions | in season | in season | in season | in season |
| squashes, summer | | in season | in season | |
| squashes, winter | | | in season | in season |
| strawberries | | in season | | |
| swede | | | in season | in season |
| sweet potatoes | | | in season | in season |
| Swiss chard | in season | | in season | in season |
| tarragon | | in season | | |
| thyme | in season | in season | in season | |
| tomatoes | | in season | in season | |
| turnips | | | in season | in season |
| watercress | in season | in season | in season | in season |
| whitecurrants | | in season | | |

# index

# acknowledgements

My thanks to all the food writers, whose
work I have read and been influenced by
over the years, but in particular to Jane
Grigson, Hugh Fearnley-Whittingstall,
Paul Waddington, Xanthe Clay and
Madhur Jaffrey. And, of course, enormous
thanks to all my friends and family for
their enthusiasm and appetites, and to
Grace Cheetham and all the team at
Duncan Baird for helping me bring
this book to fruition.